pure vegetarian

Paul Gayler

pure vegetarian

modern and stylish vegetarian cooking

photography by Gus Filgate

Kyle Cathie Limited

To all those who love food –
a constant source of joy

All recipes serve 4 unless otherwise stated

Paperback published in Great Britain in 2008 by
Kyle Cathie Limited
122 Arlington Road
London NW1 7HP
general.enquiries@kyle-cathie.com
www.kylecathie.com

First published in Great Britain in 2006

ISBN 978 1 85626 740 3

Editor Sophie Allen
Designer Vanessa Courtier
Photographer Gus Filgate
Home economist Linda Tubby
Stylist Penny Markham
Proofreader Stephanie Horner
Indexer Alex Corrin
Production by Sha Huxtable and Alice Holloway

Paul Gayler is hereby identified as the author of this work
in accordance with Section 77 of the Copyright, Designs
and Patents Act 1988.

A Cataloguing in Publication record for this title is available
from the British Library.

Colour Reproduction by SC International
Printed and bound in China by
C & C Offset Printing Company Ltd

Contents

Introduction

I wrote my first book, *Virtually Vegetarian*, over ten years ago. A celebration of vegetables and vegetarian cooking, it placed vegetables firmly centre stage. It was the beginning of the trend towards healthier eating and healthier living, with the emphasis placed on eating a good, balanced, vegetable-based diet and reducing the consumption of meat. Looking back, I suppose it was quite radical. When I started cooking professionally, it was hard, if not impossible, to find a decent vegetarian meal. So-called top restaurants concentrated on the main course – meat – and never the vegetarian option. When I became head chef at one of London's most expensive restaurants, I was happy to cater for meat eaters and vegetarians alike. Other chefs often asked me why I bothered. After all, vegetarians didn't want to eat at such grand establishments, did they? They were just a fanatical lot who didn't have enough to worry about! I saw it differently, however. Why shouldn't vegetarian dishes be interesting and imaginative?

Even nowadays, it is not unusual for high-profile chefs to talk contemptuously about vegetarians, saying they don't appreciate good food. But I have never considered them difficult to cater for. They are just customers who, for one reason or another, have decided to forsake meat and fish in their diet. Think about it for a moment. If you were to stay in a hotel and be served sausages for breakfast, toad in the hole for lunch and sausage rolls for dinner, wouldn't you feel just a little aggrieved? Isn't that how a vegetarian might feel when faced with yet another offering of the ubiquitous omelette, vegetarian lasagne or nut loaf?

I believe chefs are missing a great opportunity when they neglect to cater imaginatively for vegetarians. In recent years there has been a renewed interest in vegetarianism. While certain cultural and religious groups have practised it for centuries, now an increasing number of people are adopting it for a variety of reasons, whether economic, humanitarian or simply for better health. Following a vegetarian way of life is now far more acceptable than it once was – even, should I say, fashionable. It is worth remembering that roughly 45 per cent of the population have reduced their meat intake by choice. In my experience, putting an interesting vegetarian option on the menu appeals to a large number of non-vegetarians too.

This is my third book on vegetarian food and I have spent twenty years catering for vegetarians at the highest level. Yet I am still a meat eater, and as such I welcome the idea that everyone can enjoy vegetarian dishes. I don't believe in fad cuisines or diet regimes, simply in good food. My greatest wish is that vegetarian cuisine will one day be on an equal footing with meat and fish cookery. Great cooking is all about taste, and I firmly believe that you can achieve complex, refined flavours in vegetable dishes, as in any other kind. On a recent trip to Italy, my family and I enjoyed some wonderful vegetable dishes in restaurants – ones that sat proudly alongside meat and fish options but were not labelled vegetarian. It was simply no big deal that they didn't contain meat.

The movement towards a greener cuisine has long been coming, and I'd like to feel I've been a little instrumental in its progress. I persevered for many years in creating what I believe in. When I started to come up with vegetarian menu ideas back in 1985, the overriding challenge was to overcome the image of bland, uninspiring dishes such as stews, bakes and raw salads, which generally took so much time to make and gave so little pleasure in return. I wanted to produce vibrant, exciting meals, full of variety, colour, flavour and texture. Mine is a constantly evolving, progressive style of cooking, heavily shaped by two very different influences: classic French techniques, and my fascination for flavours from the Mediterranean and the Middle and Far East. This book reflects my thirst for knowledge, my inspiration from cuisines around the world, and my desire to see vegetarian cuisine become more mainstream by the day. With the huge variety of vegetarian ingredients now available, learning to cook without meat and fish doesn't mean reinventing the wheel, it just takes a little care and thought to achieve great tastes and textures.

In France many chefs are now championing vegetables. Alain Passard and Pierre Gagnaire, for example. Has their decision to embrace vegetarian cooking coincided with growing fears about the safety of the meat supply in Europe? I think not; more likely they are seizing the opportunity to inspire menus with a seasonal approach. The same can be applied to America, where my friend, Charlie Trotter, the great chef from Chicago, continues to break the boundaries every day. These chefs treat vegetables with the kind of reverence and respect normally given to lobster or foie gras.

I hope you will find all the recipes in this book enticing and accessible. Most of them are simple to cook, although some are slightly more sophisticated and require a little more effort. You may have to search for one or two ingredients, but this is a way to experience new flavours. You will find no tempeh, no seitan and just a few recipes for tofu, as I am not an avid lover of them. Although I am not vegetarian, the recipes respect those who choose to be so and I hope you enjoy cooking and eating them. They celebrate the extraordinary bounty of vegetarian cuisine, which has been transformed over the last twenty years from a gastronomic wilderness to a mainstream way of life that all can enjoy.

Bon Appetit!

Cooking with the seasons

From the first crisp spears of spring asparagus, tender carrots and broad beans, to the sun-ripened tomatoes and courgettes of summer, from the jewel-coloured pumpkins and squashes of autumn to earthier winter favourites such as parsnips and crisp celery, the opportunities for rich and varied vegetable dishes throughout the year are endless.

So what does 'eating seasonally' mean? Simply that vegetables usually taste best and are at their most nutritious when they have been grown at the time that Nature intended (rather than cultivated in artificial conditions) and are eaten as soon as possible after harvesting (rather than kept in storage or flown half way round the world). This way you not only get the best and freshest ingredients to work with, but pay less for them, as prices remain low with the seasonal bumper crops.

Vegetables, herbs and fruits in season are so vibrantly flavoured that even the simplest preparation yields great results. I find it rather sad that our children rarely, if at all, get the opportunity to experience the taste of real food, such as a sun-warmed strawberry straight from the plant, freshly dug carrots or an apple plucked from the tree. Unfortunately it is now so easy for us to forget about the seasons when we eat. Most supermarkets carry produce that looks and tastes the same all year round They claim that this is what customers want, but what's the point if they lack flavour?

However, on a brighter note small producers have fought back over the past ten years. There has been an upsurge in farm shops, farmers' markets and home-delivery vegetable boxes, which enable us to purchase wonderful, lovingly grown seasonal ingredients. Support these small businesses at every opportunity to ensure their survival in this world of competitive supermarket monopolies. You will find they often carry seasonal produce that is not available in supermarkets.

A brief explanation of vegetarian types

Ovo-lacto Vegetarians eliminate animal consumption in its entirety but allow the inclusion of eggs (ovo) and dairy (lacto) products. This allows a wide variety of choices for the consumer and the cook.

Lacto Vegetarians prefer not to eat eggs but base their diet around vegetables, fruits, nuts, seeds and some milk and milk-based products. It is a popular style of eating, especially in Far Eastern countries.

Vegans avoid all products of animal origin, including eggs, dairy products and sometimes honey. Catering for vegans can be more challenging, but with proper planning and forethought it is possible to come up with a good and varied menu.

Semi-Vegetarians are seen as illegitimate by true vegetarians as they, through choice, include far more vegetarian meals in their diet but still occasionally eat fish, seafood and poultry, especially chicken. Most have eliminated red meat. Can we soon expect to see the pesce vegetarian (fish eating) and the pollo vegetarian (chicken eating)? It can't be long!

Fruitarians (Microbiotic) are perhaps the most extreme of all. They consume only fruits! But this does include berries, nuts, seeds and vegetable fruits such as tomatoes, cucumbers and olives. Generally, raw fruits are preferred to cooked, thereby retaining all the vitamins, minerals and natural enzymes. Some fruitarians opt to eat grains to add variety. It's growing in popularity in America but in the UK it has not really taken off. Medical experts say that this form of eating simply cannot provide all the nutrients needed for a healthy lifestyle.

RAW eating

Rawish is the consumption of unprocessed, preferably organic, whole, plant-based foods that have never been cooked. It's ranked as one of the seven most popular diets in the world – some thirty new raw-food restaurants have sprouted up (excuse the pun!) in America and I recently noticed the first raw-food restaurant in London – but is it just another celebrity fashion statement or a way of life for many to come?

Raw foods include fruits, vegetables, nuts, seeds, grains, sprouting legumes, dried fruits, seaweeds, freshly pressed juices and purified water. They are believed to provide optimal nutrition for the body, as they contain more essential enzymes than cooked foods. Enthusiasts believe that enzymes are the life force of any food and offer numerous health benefits – improved digestion, sustained energy levels, maintaining a steady weight, reducing heart disease – all in all, a general way of feeling better about ourselves. When food is cooked, it is heated above 116ºF, the temperature at which natural enzymes are destroyed. The only 'cooking' in a raw-food diet is done in a hydrator, which dries food via hot air blowing at a temperature below 116ºF.

Following a raw diet can be time-consuming: sprouting seeds and grains, soaking nuts, drying fruits and juicing vegetables and fruits. And medical experts are sceptical about the benefits, claiming that it can be unhealthy, restrictive and limited. Many users eat only 75 per cent raw food while lightly cooking the rest. But this is not a good compromise – mixing a little cooked food with the raw produces acid in the stomach, creating digestive problems.

Although I find this diet interesting from a culinary standpoint, I have yet to be convinced of its benefits. I have included some simple raw dishes (symbolised by RAW in the title) that don't involve the use of dehydrators. They give you a feel for the freshness of this type of eating and the opportunity to make up your own mind.

Pre-dinner finger foods

In these times of increased home entertaining,

it seems to be the norm to serve a little nibble

or two along with pre-dinner drinks. Whether

served hot or cold, they are an impressive way

to start off an evening. A good tip to remember

is to keep them small, simple and easy to

prepare and eat. In this chapter, I hope that you

will discover some delightful and imaginative

dishes that can be prepared with confidence

and are guaranteed to whet the appetite.

Steamed oriental buns

These delicate Malaysian-style buns are best made fresh, although they can be frozen raw and baked when needed. You may wish to serve some extra-sweet chilli sauce on the side as a dip.

for the dough

300g '00' flour
15g baking powder
15g caster sugar
15ml vegetable oil
180ml warm water

for the filling

10ml sesame oil
450g shiitake mushrooms, chopped
1/2 garlic clove, crushed
15g sugar
60g peanut butter
15ml hoisin sauce
30ml sweet chilli sauce
2 tablespoons chopped fresh coriander

makes 16 buns

For the dough, sift the dry ingredients into a bowl, stir in the oil and water, mix to a soft dough and shape into a ball. Knead on a lightly floured surface for about 3–4 minutes until smooth and pliable. Return to the bowl, cover with a tea towel and leave to stand for 10–15 minutes.

For the filling, heat the sesame oil in a wok or small frying pan, add the mushrooms and garlic and stir-fry for 2–3 minutes. Add the remaining ingredients, mix well together and cook until the mixture is thick and sticky in texture. Remove to a bowl and leave to cool.

Roll out the dough and, using an 8cm cookie cutter, cut out sixteen rounds. Flatten each round with the palm of your hand to form thin rounds (about 2mm thick). Place a good tablespoon of the mushroom filling in the centre of each round, gather up the edges and twist firmly to secure the filling. Place the buns (gathered-side up) onto a tinfoil- or paper-lined bamboo steamer, ensuring the buns are not touching. Place over a wok or pan of simmering water for 15 minutes or until firm. Serve warm.

Cajun mozzarella and ricotta fritters

Adding cajun spices to the cheese mixture really gives the fritters a lift and is an ideal way to get the gastric juices flowing.

400g ricotta cheese, well drained

$^1/_2$ teaspoon garlic powder

$^1/_2$ teaspoon cayenne

1 teaspoon smoked paprika (or paprika)

1 tablespoon chopped fresh oregano leaves

1 tablespoon fresh thyme leaves

200g dried white breadcrumbs

200g buffalo mozzarella, patted dry and cut into 1cm dice

50g plain flour

2 free-range eggs, beaten

100g fine cornmeal (polenta)

vegetable oil for deep-frying

salt and cracked black pepper

for the Virgin Mary dip

1 teaspoon Worcestershire sauce

100ml tomato ketchup

drop of Tabasco sauce

1 teaspoon creamed horseradish

salt and freshly ground black pepper

makes 16 fritters

Place the drained ricotta in a bowl and add the garlic powder, spices and fresh herbs; season well with salt and cracked black pepper. Stir in half the breadcrumbs, then add the dried mozzarella. Divide the mixture into sixteen small balls, place on a plate and refrigerate for 1 hour to firm up.

For the dip, combine all the ingredients together in a bowl and season to taste.

Remove the cheese balls from the fridge, pass them through the flour, then into the beaten eggs and then into a mixture of the remaining breadcrumbs and the fine cornmeal. Roll them individually in the palm of your hand to obtain good round shapes.

Heat the vegetable oil to 180°C/350°F and add the fritters a few at a time, being careful not to overcrowd the pan. Deep-fry for 1–2 minutes until golden, remove and drain on kitchen paper. Pierce each ball with a cocktail stick and place on a serving dish with some Virgin Mary dip on the side.

Mini aubergine spring rolls

These spring rolls are extremely tasty and the ideal finger food with drinks. They can be made in advance and frozen to take a little stress out of entertaining. Serve with soy sauce.

4 tablespoons sunflower oil

2 teaspoons sesame oil

2 medium-sized aubergines, cut into 1cm dice

1 shallot, finely chopped

1 small garlic clove, crushed

1 tablespoon sweet chilli sauce

2 tablespoons Indonesian soy sauce (kecap manis)

2 tablespoons chopped fresh coriander

12 spring roll wrappers

4 tablespoons groundnut oil

salt and freshly ground black pepper

makes 12 rolls

Heat the sunflower oil and sesame oil in a frying pan over a moderate heat, add the diced aubergine, shallot and garlic and stir-fry for 5–6 minutes until golden and tender. Place into a bowl and leave to cool. When cool, add the chilli sauce, kecap manis and chopped coriander; season to taste.

Lay the spring roll wrappers out on a work surface and place an equal amount of aubergine filling at one end of each wrapper. Roll up tightly, folding in the sides to secure the filling. Brush the end of each wrapper with a little water to seal.

Heat the groundnut oil in a frying pan and fry the spring rolls for 4–5 minutes, turning them regularly until golden all over. Drain on kitchen paper and serve with soy sauce.

Mini tortilla wraps

These little wraps of flour tortillas are packed with flavour and have been served as vegetarian canapés at The Lanesborough for more years than I care to remember.

25g unsalted butter
1 small red chilli, deseeded and finely chopped
150g baby spinach, washed and well drained
150g cooked black beans, lightly crushed
1 small ripe mango, peeled and cut into 1cm dice
75g freshly grated vegetarian cheddar cheese
2 flour tortillas
90ml sour cream
salt and freshly ground black pepper

makes 12 mini wraps

Melt the butter in a frying pan, throw in the chilli and spinach and cook over a high heat for 1 minute. Add the lightly crushed black beans and mango and toss the whole mix together; season to taste. Remove from the heat, add the cheese and mix well. Set aside.

Heat another large frying pan and, when hot, add the tortillas one at a time and toast them on both sides for 10–15 seconds until lightly charred. Lay out the tortillas on a flat surface, fill each one with equal quantities of the filling, then roll them up tightly into wraps. Trim the ends off the tortillas and then cut each one into six small equal wraps. Serve with the sour cream.

Warm mini cocktail sandwiches

Based on the English tea sandwich, these tasty bite-sized morsels come from further afield. They combine freshness and simplicity for serving with pre-dinner drinks. And they can be prepared beforehand and cooked when needed.

Tapenade with sunblush tomato toasts

Tapenade is an olive paste that can be made easily, but you can find some delicious ready-made versions in good delicatessens.

50g unsalted butter, softened
25g rocket, roughly chopped
4 slices of white sandwich bread
2 tablespoons tapenade
50g sunblush tomatoes, drained and dried
40g fontina (or emmental) cheese, grated
30ml olive oil
salt and freshly ground black pepper

makes 12 squares

Mix the butter and rocket and season lightly. Spread the rocket butter on both sides of each bread slice. Spread a layer of tapenade onto two of the slices of bread. Top with sunblush tomatoes, covering the whole surface. Scatter over the fontina cheese, then close up the sandwiches with the other two pieces of bread, pressing down gently to make them compact.

Heat the olive oil in a frying pan over a moderate heat and fry the sandwiches for about 2 minutes on each side until golden all over. Remove and drain on kitchen paper. Using a sharp knife, remove the crusts and cut each sandwich into six small squares. Serve immediately.

Crushed artichoke and goat's cheese pesto toasts

If you can, buy your artichoke hearts from a good Italian delicatessen for that superior flavour.

50g unsalted butter, softened

4 slices of white sandwich bread

4 marinated artichoke hearts, drained and dried

2 tablespoons soft goat's cheese

1 tablespoon pesto (home-made or bought)

1 teaspoon chopped fresh oregano

2 tablespoons freshly grated castelli vegetalia
  (parmesan-style cheese)

30ml olive oil

salt and freshly ground black pepper

makes 12 squares

Spread the butter on both sides of each bread slice. In a bowl, break down the marinated artichokes with a fork. Add the goat's cheese, pesto and oregano; season well to taste.

Carefully spread out the mixture onto two of the buttered slices, then close up the sandwiches with the other two pieces of bread, pressing down gently to make them compact. Sprinkle them both liberally all over with grated parmesan.

Heat the olive oil in a frying pan over a moderate heat and fry the sandwiches for about 2 minutes on each side until golden all over. Remove and drain on kitchen paper. Using a sharp knife, remove the crusts and cut each sandwich into six small squares. Serve immediately.

Wild mushroom and taleggio croque monsieurs

Taleggio is a wonderful Italian cheese that goes so well with wild mushrooms.

60ml olive oil

75g assorted wild mushrooms, cleaned and sliced

1 garlic clove, crushed

1 tablespoon chopped fresh flat-leaf parsley

50g unsalted butter, softened

4 slices of white sandwich bread

50g taleggio cheese, thinly sliced

salt and freshly ground black pepper

makes 12 squares

Heat half the olive oil in a frying pan over a moderate heat, add the mushrooms and garlic and fry until golden and tender. Add the parsley and season well to taste. Remove and leave to cool.

Spread the butter on both sides of each bread slice. Divide the mushrooms equally and place onto two slices of the bread. Top the mushrooms with slices of the taleggio, then close up the sandwiches with the other two slices of bread, pressing down gently to make them compact.

Heat the remaining oil in another frying pan, add the sandwiches and fry for 2–3 minutes on each side until golden all over. Remove and drain on kitchen paper. Using a sharp knife, remove the crusts and cut each sandwich into six small squares. Serve immediately.

Cream cheese, beetroot and truffle tarts

The use of creamy cheese and sweet beetroot is a particular favourite of mine because it is relatively cheap, easy to prepare and looks beautiful.

420g prepared short pastry

2 medium-sized roasted beetroots (see page 77)

1 teaspoon balsamic vinegar

2 tablespoons maple syrup

125g good-quality cream cheese

2 tablespoons snipped fresh chives (plus more
   for garnishing)

1 tablespoon truffle oil

salt and freshly ground black pepper

12 mini-tartlet cases

makes 12 tarts

Preheat the oven to 190°C/375°F/gas mark 5. Roll out the pastry very thinly and, using a 5cm biscuit cutter, cut out twelve rounds of pastry. Line twelve tartlet cases with the rounds and cook in the oven for 10 minutes until golden. Leave to cool. (These may be prepared in advance and stored in an airtight container.)

Cut the beetroots into small dice and place in a pan with the vinegar and maple syrup. Cook over a low heat for 4–5 minutes so that they become lightly caramelised and have a sweet and sour flavour. Remove and leave to cool.

Mix the cream cheese with the chives and season to taste.

Fill each tartlet case with cream cheese, then top with a spoonful of beetroot. Drizzle a little truffle oil over each tartlet, garnish with some snipped chives and serve.

Appetisers

Although all constituents of a great meal
are significant, one must never forget the
importance of a well prepared appetiser. It must
be beautiful to look at and ultimately light and
flavourful, whilst leaving room for the dishes to
follow. Inevitably it sets the tone of what's to
come, but more importantly it stimulates the
palate and entices and delights the diner.
Creating interesting appetisers opens up a
world of culinary adventures – all it takes is a
little imagination.

Vegetables à la grecque
with avocado cheese and herb-scented juices

A light and tasty vegetable dish, simply presented in the Greek style,
accompanied with a fragrant herb sauce made from the cooking juices –
ideal for the summertime.

for the avocado cheese

1/2 avocado, preferably Haas variety

100g feta cheese

juice of 1/2 lemon

salt and freshly ground black pepper

4 tablespoons white wine vinegar

1 garlic clove, crushed

juice of 1 lemon

1 teaspoon coriander seeds, crushed

sprig of fresh thyme

8 tablespoons olive oil

250g baby courgettes, halved lengthways

16 green asparagus tips, peeled and trimmed

4 white asparagus tips, peeled and trimmed

20g fresh flat-leaf parsley leaves

30g fresh basil leaves

40g fresh celery leaves

salt and freshly ground black pepper

For the avocado cheese, place the avocado flesh and cheese in a food processor and blend to a smooth paste. Remove to a bowl, add the lemon juice and season to taste. Cover the bowl with clingfilm and refrigerate until required.

Heat 150ml water with the vinegar, garlic, lemon juice, coriander seeds and thyme in a pan, bring to the boil and simmer for 15 minutes. Add half the oil. Add the courgettes and asparagus and cook until just tender, retaining a little crunch to them. Remove and leave to cool, reserving the cooking liquid.

Place the parsley, basil and celery leaves in a food processor and blend, adding enough of the cooking liquid to form a light purée. Add the remaining olive oil, blend again, remove and season to taste.

Pour a little of the sauce on each serving plate, add the cooked vegetables and top with a quenelle of avocado cheese (using a spoon or ice-cream scoop). Garnish with the coriander seeds and thyme leaves from the cooking liquid.

Haloumi tandoori
with carrot pachadi

I am a great lover of the foods of Asia – vibrant and flavour-packed dishes that excite the palate and all the senses. The haloumi cheese skewers are more at home in Central Europe than India, but it really works well with the tandoori spices.

for the haloumi marinade

2 garlic cloves, crushed

25g chopped fresh coriander

2 shallots, chopped

2 red peppers, deseeded and chopped

juice of 1 lime

1 teaspoon paprika

2 tablespoons tandoori paste

500g haloumi cheese

little olive oil

for the carrot pachadi

4 tablespoons olive oil

12 curry leaves

pinch of black mustard seeds

1 garlic clove

pinch of salt

1 small red chilli, deseeded and finely chopped

juice of 1 lemon

1 large carrot, peeled and finely shredded

1 red onion, thinly sliced

4 wooden or bamboo skewers
   (soaked in water for 24 hours)

For the haloumi marinade, place all the ingredients except the tandoori paste in a food processor and blend until smooth. Add the paste, blend again and transfer into a large bowl. Cut the haloumi into large blocks, place in a bowl and toss well with the marinade. Cover with clingfilm and refrigerate overnight.

Skewer the haloumi onto the wooden skewers to form a kebab. Heat a little olive oil in a large frying pan or alternatively on a grill pan over a moderate heat. Cook the kebabs for 1–2 minutes on each side. (Do not overcook them as haloumi can become hard when overcooked.)

While they cook, heat the 4 tablespoons of olive oil in a small frying pan over a moderate heat and fry the curry leaves and mustard seeds for 20–30 seconds.

Crush the garlic in a mortar with a little salt and chilli. Add the lemon juice, curry leaves and mustard seeds. Transfer to a bowl, add the shredded carrot and onion and toss well together. Serve with the kebabs.

PG TIPS   I also occasionally serve some thick yogurt on the side, which I think goes well with this dish.

Seaweed daikon wraps

with ginger and sesame dipping sauce – RAW

A simple and healthy raw dish of marinated shredded vegetables wrapped in thin white radish slices. They are star attractions in Vietnamese homes and can be made with all manner of fillings. Yuzu is an unusual citrus fruit with a flavour that is a cross between a tangerine and a lime. Substitute with fresh lime juice if you need to.

1 white radish (daikon)

2 tablespoons maple syrup

25g raw cashews, finely chopped

2 tablespoons yuzu juice (or lime juice)

1 avocado, halved, stoned and cut into 1cm dice

25g hijiki (or wakame) seaweed, soaked in hot water for
*   15–20 minutes, drained and dried*

1/2 cucumber, deseeded and thinly shredded

1 red pepper, deseeded and thinly shredded

1 carrot, peeled and thinly sliced

1 small mango, peeled and thinly shredded

25g fresh coriander leaves

25g fresh mint leaves

25g fresh basil leaves

50g purple shiso cress (if available)

salt and freshly ground black pepper

for the dipping sauce

5 tablespoons rice wine vinegar

2 tablespoons soy sauce

1 stick of lemongrass, outer casing discarded,
*   finely chopped*

1 tablespoon pickled ginger, chopped, juice reserved

2 tablespoons ginger juice (from above)

1 tablespoon peanut oil

1 tablespoon sesame oil

1 tablespoon yuzu juice (or lime juice)

salt and freshly ground black pepper

makes 12 wraps

Peel the white radish and slice very thinly lengthways using a kitchen mandolin (a similar result can be achieved using a broad-bladed swivel-headed vegetable peeler) and set aside.

In a large bowl, mix together the maple syrup, cashews and yuzu juice. Add the avocado, seaweed, vegetables, mango and herbs, except the shiso cress, and toss gently together; season to taste.

To assemble the rolls, trim the radish slices to 2–2$1/2$cm strips in length. Lay two strips alongside each other, slightly overlapping, place a round of the mixture at one end. Add the shiso cress on top, then roll up firmly to form neat rolls. Place on a large plate. The mixture should make twelve wraps in total. Keep chilled.

For the dipping sauce, combine the vinegar, soy sauce, lemongrass, ginger and juice in a food processor. With the machine running, slowly drizzle in the oils and yuzu or lime juice and adjust the seasoning.

Place the wraps on a serving plate (cut them in half if you prefer) and serve with the dipping sauce alongside.

PG TIPS   Another great dipping sauce for these wraps can be made by simply blending together 1 avocado with 1 chopped spring onion and the juice of half a lemon. Then add 1 tablespoon of rice wine vinegar, 4 tablespoons of coconut milk and blend to a purée. Remove and fold through with 1 tablespoon of sweet chilli sauce before serving.

Stuffed courgette flowers

with chickpeas, new potatoes and lemon olive oil

Chefs eagerly await the summer and the arrival of the first courgette flowers to adorn their tables. If you are not lucky enough to grow your own or know someone who does, they can be found in specialist shops or country farm shops.

12 courgette blossoms (female, small courgette attached)
1 tablespoon olive oil
1 small onion, chopped
1 garlic clove, crushed
1 red pepper, roasted, deseeded and chopped
100g chickpea flour (gram flour)
200g cooked chickpeas (tinned are fine)
1 teaspoon chopped fresh rosemary
1 litre vegetable oil
salt and freshly ground black pepper

for the batter

1 free-range egg
50g plain flour (plus a little extra for coating)
4 tablespoons cold water

for the salad

300g new potatoes, scrubbed
50g watercress, leaves only
50g rocket leaves
2 hard-boiled free-range eggs, shelled

for the lemon olive oil

100ml extra-virgin olive oil
50g stoned black olives
zest and juice of 1/2 lemon

serves 4–6

Firstly clean the courgettes by gently washing the flowers and drying the outside.

For the stuffing, heat the olive oil in a pan, add the onion, garlic and pepper and cook over a low heat for 4–5 minutes until soft. In a separate pan bring to the boil 200ml water, pour in the chickpea flour and stir until smooth, lower the heat and cook for 2–3 minutes. In a food processor blend the chickpeas with the onion, garlic and pepper to a coarse paste. Add the chickpea flour mixture and rosemary and season. Leave to cool.

For the batter, beat the eggs in a bowl, stir in the flour, then gradually add the water to make a smooth consistency. Set aside.

For the salad, cook the potatoes in plenty of boiling salted water until tender. Drain and leave to cool to room temperature. Slice the potatoes and place in a bowl, add the watercress and rocket. Chop the egg whites and pass the yolks through a sieve and add to the salad. Set aside.

Fill the courgette flowers with the chickpea mixture and twist the ends to secure the inner filling. Heat the vegetable oil to 170ºC/325ºF. Dip the flowers into a little flour, then into the batter and fry in the hot oil for about 1–2 minutes until golden brown. Drain on the kitchen paper.

For the lemon olive oil, mix all the ingredients together in a bowl. Toss the salad with the dressing and place onto four individual plates. Place the courgette flowers on top and serve.

Poached egg on potato muffins
with watercress hollandaise

Spring heralds the arrival of vitamin-packed watercress, hailed today as a superhero amongst salad leaves. However, the use of watercress in hot dishes should never be overlooked – here it makes an interesting addition to the well loved hollandaise sauce. A great dish that can be enjoyed for breakfast, lunch or brunch.

75g unsalted butter

2 small leeks, trimmed and thinly shredded

350g hot mashed potato (made with floury potatoes)

25g freshly grated castelli vegetalia (parmesan-style cheese)

1 free-range egg, beaten

75g plain flour (plus a little extra for coating)

4 tablespoons vegetable oil

2 tablespoons vinegar

4 large free-range eggs

watercress to garnish (optional)

1 tablespoon truffle oil

salt and freshly ground black pepper

for the watercress hollandaise

3 large free-range egg yolks at room temperature

juice of 1/2 lemon

85g watercress, leaves only

225g unsalted butter

salt and freshly ground black pepper

Melt 50g butter in a pan, add the leeks and cook over a low heat for 8–10 minutes or until tender.

Place the hot mashed potato in a bowl, beat in the remaining butter and the cheese and season well. Beat in the egg and flour. Separate the potato mixture into four equal portions and, with floured hands, form the portions into balls and then make an indentation in the centre of each ball. Place a good spoonful of the leeks into each indentation, then reform the balls to totally enclose the filling. Flatten each ball to make a flat cake about 2cm deep, then coat each one in a little flour. Set aside.

For the hollandaise, place the egg yolks, 2 tablespoons of water, the lemon juice, watercress and a little salt and pepper in a food processor and blend until just combined. Heat the butter in a pan to just under boiling point. With the motor running, gently pour in the butter through the funnel at the top, leaving the milky residues behind – the sauce should be creamy and thick. Adjust the seasoning to taste and keep warm.

Heat the vegetable oil in a frying pan over a moderate heat and fry the potato muffins for 3–4 minutes on each side until golden. Meanwhile poach the eggs.

Bring 1 litre water with the vinegar to the boil. Reduce the heat, crack in the eggs, two at a time, and simmer gently for 2–3 minutes or until the eggs are just set but still a little soft. Carefully remove them from the water with a slotted spoon and drain well on kitchen paper.

Place the potato muffins on four plates, carefully top each with a poached egg, a grinding of black pepper and a spoonful or two of watercress hollandaise. Garnish with the watercress, if using, then finally drizzle over a little truffle oil.

Pan-roasted asparagus

with truffled eggs sunny-side-up

If you are ever lucky enough to have a freshly dug white Piedmont truffle at hand, then this is the dish for it. The combination of butter-fried egg, asparagus and truffle is a dish of simplicity but utmost sophistication. White truffles are found from late autumn to early winter – they are extremely expensive and highly regarded.

for the gremolata

25g unsalted butter

75g fresh white breadcrumbs

2 tablespoons chopped fresh flat-leaf parsley

1 tablespoon freshly grated castelli vegetalia
(parmesan-style cheese)

24 fresh green asparagus, peeled and trimmed

45g unsalted butter

4 large free-range eggs

1 small white truffle

salt and freshly cracked black pepper

For the gremolata, heat the butter in a pan and, when foaming, add the breadcrumbs and parsley and cook until lightly golden and toasted. Add the castelli vegetalia, remove and leave to cool.

Cook the asparagus in boiling salted water for 3–4 minutes or until tender (according to their size), remove and drain well. In a small non-stick frying pan, melt the butter and fry the eggs. Place the asparagus onto four serving plates and top with a fried egg. Season with salt and freshly cracked black pepper. Sprinkle over the gremolata. Finally shave the white truffle over the top and serve immediately.

PG TIPS   You could use a teaspoon of white truffle oil (which is far less expensive!) and drizzle it over the eggs instead of the fresh white truffle – your pocket will be better for it but the flavour won't, I'm afraid.

Rosemary-grilled goat's cheese
with warm apricot relish and pistachio oil

Tinned apricots are best for this relish because they are cooked for a short time to retain their natural flavours. It has a tangy sweet and sour flavour, which works wonderfully with the taste of rosemary-grilled cheese.

4 tablespoons double cream

1 teaspoon fresh rosemary leaves, roughly chopped

4 small round goat's cheese (eg. crottin chavignol)

2 small crisp bread rolls, each cut into 4 thin
 slices lengthways

extra-virgin olive oil for brushing

75g fresh buckler leaf sorrel or watercress

for the apricot relish

1 small onion, finely chopped

60ml white wine vinegar

2 tablespoons brown sugar

425g tinned apricots, chopped and juice reserved

2 tablespoons raisins, soaked until plump in warm
 water, drained

for the pistachio oil

75g good-quality very green pistachio nuts

100ml extra-virgin olive oil

Preheat a grill to its highest setting. Place the cream and chopped rosemary in a small bowl and lightly whip with a small whisk or fork until it begins to thicken. Set aside. Cut the cheeses in half horizontally and top each of them with a thick smear of the rosemary cream. Place on a plate and refrigerate until needed.

For the relish, place the onion, vinegar and sugar in a small pan and cook gently for 6–8 minutes to form a light syrup. Add the chopped apricots, their juices and the raisins and cook for 5–8 minutes or until the apricots become thick and jam-like in consistency. Remove and keep warm.

For the pistachio oil, place the pistachios and oil in a blender and blitz for about 1 minute until smooth. Remove and strain through a muslin cloth (ideally) or a fine strainer.

Toast the thin bread roll slices under the grill on both sides, then brush them liberally with olive oil. Place the cheeses on a grill pan and place under the grill, as close as you can bear to the heat itself, until they are golden and glazed beautifully. Place 1 spoonful of relish on each toasted bread slice and top with a slice of goat's cheese. Garnish the cheeses with some buckler leaf sorrel or watercress and a drizzle of the pistachio oil.

Vine-baked camembert
with pepper-cranberry jelly and fennel salsa

Putting these vine leaves in the oven imparts an almost lemony taste to
the cheese, while the peppercorns add a pleasant kick. Serve with plenty
of grilled country bread.

for the pepper-cranberry jelly

227g jar cranberry jelly

1 teaspoon green peppercorns in brine, drained and
* lightly crushed*

4g vege-gel

1 camembert cheese, cut into 6 equal wedges

1/2 teaspoon olive oil

1/2 teaspoon coarsely cracked black pepper

12 vine leaves in brine, drained

for the fennel salsa

4 tablespoons extra-virgin olive oil

1 head fennel, trimmed and cut into 1cm dice

1 garlic clove, crushed

1 tablespoon balsamic vinegar

10g unsalted butter

juice of 1/2 lemon

2 spring onions, chopped

1 tablespoon chopped fresh coriander

4 sun-dried tomatoes in oil, drained and chopped

salt and freshly ground black pepper

serves 6

For the jelly, melt the cranberry jelly in a pan over a moderate heat. Stir in the crushed green peppercorns and cook for 1 minute. Sprinkle over the vege-gel, stir in and heat until the jelly thickens. Pour into a small bowl and refrigerate overnight or until set.

Preheat the oven to 190°C/375°F/gas mark 5. Brush the camembert wedges with a little olive oil and a little seasoning of black pepper.

Rinse the vine leaves under cold running water, then dry them in a dry cloth. Place two overlapping vine leaves on a flat surface, then set one wedge of cheese in the centre of the overlapping vine leaves and bring up the sides to neatly wrap the cheese. Prepare the remaining five wedges in the same manner. Place the wrapped cheeses on a large baking sheet and set aside.

For the fennel salsa, heat half the oil in a pan over a moderate heat, add the fennel and cook for 3–4 minutes until softened. Transfer to a bowl, add the remaining ingredients and season to taste. Leave to cool.

Place the cheeses in the oven for 4–5 minutes. Place a baked camembert on each serving plate, garnish with a good spoon of jelly and pour around some of the fennel salsa. Serve immediately.

Marinated oyster mushrooms

with basil and ginger

You can use shiitake or chestnut mushrooms instead. Don't chill before
serving as the delicate marinating juices dilute the flavour.

1cm piece of root ginger, peeled and chopped

2 garlic cloves, peeled and thinly sliced

2 green chillies, deseeded and thinly sliced

400g oyster mushrooms

2 tablespoons groundnut or vegetable oil

2 tablespoons light soy sauce

1 teaspoon palm sugar or brown sugar

1 tablespoon fresh lemon juice

30g thai basil (or sweet basil)

coarse sea salt and freshly ground black pepper

Place the chopped ginger, garlic and chilli in a mortar, add a little salt and crush lightly with the pestle to form a smooth paste. Trim the oyster mushrooms and clean them of any dirt with a damp cloth, then cut them into bite-sized pieces if necessary.

Heat the oil in a wok or large frying pan and, when hot, add the paste and cook for 20–30 seconds to infuse the oil. Throw in the mushrooms and cook for 3–4 minutes. Add the soy sauce and sugar and cook for a further 1 minute. Adjust the seasoning, add the lemon juice and basil, toss together and remove from the heat. Transfer to a bowl and leave to cool before serving at room temperature.

Chinese-fried asparagus

with miso and sesame

An oriental way of enjoying asparagus that takes only minutes to make.

1 tablespoon sesame seeds

2 tablespoons vegetable or sunflower oil

2.5cm piece of root ginger, peeled and grated

1 garlic clove, crushed

1 teaspoon white miso

2 tablespoons mirin

24 asparagus, peeled, trimmed and cut into 5cm pieces

1 teaspoon sugar

cracked black pepper

2 teaspoons sesame oil

2 tablespoons soy sauce

Heat a large frying pan or wok, add the sesame seeds and dry-fry over a high heat for 1 minute or until golden. Set aside. Return the pan to the heat, add the oil, ginger, garlic, miso and mirin and mix well. Add the asparagus and stir-fry for 2–3 minutes or until almost tender. Sprinkle over the sugar and a little cracked black pepper and stir-fry for a further 1 minute.

Divide onto four serving plates and spoon over the sesame oil, soy sauce and sesame seeds. Serve immediately.

Spanish romescu baby leeks

A simple dish using leeks poached in an aromatic broth, lifted with a purée of red peppers, chilli and almonds. It is ideally eaten at room temperature to appreciate it at its best. Artichokes are also good served this way. Serve with lots of crusty bread to mop up the wonderful juices.

for the purée

4 tablespoons extra-virgin olive oil

1 slice of country-style loaf, crusts removed

juice of 1/4 lemon

2 garlic cloves, crushed

90g almonds, peeled and toasted

2 red peppers, roasted and peeled

1 teaspoon tomato purée

1 red chilli

100g ripe tomatoes

4 tablespoons extra-virgin olive oil

1 tablespoon dry white wine

1/2 teaspoon sugar

1 bay leaf

sprig of thyme

sprig of rosemary

1 garlic clove, crushed

4 coriander seeds, crushed

500g baby leeks, trimmed, but left whole

1 tablespoon chopped fresh flat-leaf parsley

salt and freshly ground black pepper

For the purée, heat the olive oil in a frying pan over a moderate heat, add the bread and fry until golden. Transfer to a food processor and add the lemon juice, garlic and almonds and blend to a smooth paste. Add the roasted peppers, tomato purée, chilli and tomatoes and blend again until smooth and creamy in texture.

Place the oil, wine, sugar, bay leaf, thyme, rosemary, garlic and coriander seeds and 600ml water in a pan, bring to the boil and simmer for 10 minutes. Add the leeks and simmer for 15–20 minutes or until the leeks are tender. Remove the leeks and place them in a dish. Remove the bay leaf, thyme and rosemary from the cooking liquid. Add the purée to the cooking liquid, whisk well together and season to taste.

Place the leeks on a serving dish, pour the romescu broth over the leeks and leave to cool. Serve at room temperature or cold, garnished with the chopped parsley.

Stuffed riesling-braised artichokes
with herb-infused oil

Serving fresh artichokes is always an impressive affair, but they do need a lot of preparation, which is I feel, the reason why they are not as popular to cook at home as they should be. They can be prepared up to the filling stage well in advance, then finished when needed.

4 globe artichokes, about 300g each

2 lemons, halved

4 tablespoons olive oil

1 small onion, finely chopped

1 garlic clove, crushed

125g wild (or cultivated) mushrooms, coarsely chopped

150g fresh spinach

4 tablespoons double cream

25g chopped walnuts

30g freshly grated castelli vegetalia (parmesan-style cheese)

25g fresh breadcrumbs

100ml Riesling wine or other dry white wine

large sprig of lemon thyme (or thyme)

40g unsalted butter

1/2 teaspoon lemon zest

50g fresh herbs (tarragon, chervil, chives, flat-leaf parsley)

salt and freshly ground black pepper

Preheat the oven to 180°C/350°F/gas mark 4. Using a large sharp knife, trim about 5cm from the top of each artichoke and, using kitchen scissors, cut off the thorny top third of the leaves. Squeeze the lemons into a large pot of lightly salted boiling water, add the artichokes and top with a plate which will keep the artichokes submerged in the water as they cook. Cook for 18–20 minutes or until the outer leaves of the artichokes can be pulled out easily. Remove the artichokes with a slotted spoon, let them drain and cool upside down on a kitchen towel. Retain the cooking liquid.

To prepare the stuffing, heat 3 tablespoons of the oil in a frying pan, add the onion, garlic and mushrooms and cook over a moderate heat for 2–3 minutes until softened. Add the spinach and cook until all the water has evaporated. Add the cream and walnuts and cook for a further 2 minutes. Place in a food processor and blend until smooth. Add the castelli vegetalia and breadcrumbs and mix well to bind. Transfer back to the pan and cook for 1 minute. Season to taste and remove to a bowl to cool.

Remove the tiny hairy chokes from each artichoke with a teaspoon. Fill the centre of each artichoke with the stuffing, pressing it down well into the base. Place the stuffed artichokes in a suitable size casserole dish, pour over the white wine, the remaining olive oil and 300ml reserved artichoke cooking liquid, tuck in the lemon thyme and place in the oven to bake for 15–20 minutes.

Place the artichokes in four individual shallow bowls or soup plates. Strain the cooking liquid into a small pan, bring to the boil and then simmer until reduced in volume. Whisk in the butter, lemon zest and herbs, season to taste, and pour around the artichokes to serve.

Emmental and tomato French toasts

with green bean and shallot vinaigrette

A savoury French toast appetiser idea; the same principle could apply to
many other delicious fillings on the same lines, such as goat's cheese
and olives. Always choose the best quality bread you can for these
French toasts.

50g unsalted butter, softened

8 slices of thin white bread

150g vegetarian emmental cheese, thinly sliced

*2 tablespoons good-quality pesto sauce (bought or home-
    made – see PG TIPS page 103)*

100g sunblush tomatoes, drained, oil reserved

100ml single cream

1 large free-range egg

30g finely grated castelli vegetalia (parmesan-style cheese)

little clarified butter (see PG TIPS page 171) or olive oil

salt, freshly ground black pepper and ground nutmeg

for the bean and shallot vinaigrette

200g cooked French beans

2 shallots, finely chopped

6 black olives, stoned and finely chopped

1/2 garlic clove, crushed

1 red chilli, deseeded and finely chopped

4 tablespoons reserved oil from sunblush tomatoes

juice of 1/2 lemon

salt and freshly ground black pepper

Spread the butter on both sides of each bread slice, top four of the slices with
emmental cheese and layer over the pesto. Scatter some sunblush tomatoes over
the pesto then close up the sandwiches with the remaining slices of buttered bread,
pressing down firmly to make them compact. Cut out each sandwich into circles
using a 1.5cm diameter cutter.

In a shallow tray, whisk together the cream, egg and castelli vegetalia; add a little
seasoning of salt, pepper and nutmeg. Heat a large non-stick frying pan with the
clarified butter or oil and when it's fairly hot pass the sandwiches through the cream
mixture, shaking off any excess, and place into the pan. Cook over a moderate heat
for 2 minutes on each side until golden in colour.

Meanwhile, for the vinaigrette, place the French beans and chopped shallots in a
bowl, add the remaining ingredients, toss well together and season to taste. Place the
salad on four serving plates, top with the French toasts and serve immediately.

PG TIPS   Vegetarian emmental cheese is available from leading stores. You can also
use vegetarian gouda but it is not so easily accessible.

Raw and cooked porcini mushrooms
with garlic truffle cream and cheese cracknel

A lovely contrast of raw and cooked porcini mushrooms – the king of the mushroom kingdom. They are served with a delicately infused garlic and truffle cream, and feather-light cheese wafers, which are fantastic served with all manner of dishes especially risotto, pasta and salads.

for the cheese cracknel

1 tablespoon plain flour

90g freshly grated castelli vegetalia (parmesan-style cheese)

1 teaspoon unsalted butter, softened

for the garlic truffle cream

4 garlic cloves

100ml milk

5 tablespoons double cream

1 teaspoon white truffle oil

20g finely grated castelli vegetalia (parmesan-style cheese)

salt and freshly ground black pepper

475g fresh porcini mushrooms, cleaned

1 small garlic clove, crushed

1 teaspoon fresh thyme leaves

100ml extra-virgin olive oil

zest and juice of 1/2 lemon

100g rocket leaves

salt and freshly ground black pepper

For the cheese cracknel, place the flour and castelli vegetalia in a small bowl and gently rub together with your fingers. Heat a small non-stick frying pan over a moderate heat and add the butter. Sprinkle a heaped tablespoon into the pan, press down with a fork into a thin round layer and leave to cook for 15–20 seconds until the cheese bubbles. Remove with a palette knife and place to one side to cool. Prepare all the mix in the same way.

For the cream, place the garlic and milk in a small pan and gently cook for 15 minutes until the garlic is very soft. Add the cream and transfer to a small food processor and blend until smooth. Place in a bowl and leave to cool. Add the truffle oil, castelli vegetalia and season to taste.

Divide the mushrooms equally and, with a sharp knife, cut approximately 1–2cm off the base of each stem. Cut half the mushrooms into 1cm thick slices and the other into 4mm slices. Place the thicker slices into a bowl, add a little salt, the garlic, thyme and half the olive oil. Toss carefully together and set aside. Heat a ridged grill pan over a high heat and, when smoking, carefully place the mushroom slices on the grill and cook for 2–3 minutes, turning them carefully, until golden and caramelised.

Meanwhile place the smaller mushroom slices in another bowl, pour over the remaining olive oil, lemon zest and juice and season well.

Quickly arrange the grilled and raw mushrooms on four serving plates, toss the rocket leaves with the garlic truffle cream and place in the centre of each plate. Garnish the salad with some crispy cheese cracknel and serve immediately.

Avocado salsa rolls
with hot limes

In this recipe all the ingredients of the well loved guacamole come into play, plus a few others using Chef's poetic licence. These little rolls not only look wonderful but are packed with great Mexican flavours.

175g dried black beans (turtle beans)
1 small red onion, finely chopped
4 plum tomatoes, chopped
150g sweetcorn (tinned are fine)
1 mango, peeled and chopped
50g chopped fresh coriander
4 firm but ripe avocados (preferably Fuerte variety)
few small rocket leaves

for the dressing
1 garlic clove, crushed
1 small red chilli, deseeded and finely chopped
juice of 1 lemon
75ml olive oil
pinch of ground cumin
1 tablespoon maple syrup
2 limes, halved

Soak the black beans in cold water overnight, rinse under cold water and drain. Place them in a pan, cover with water and bring to the boil. Reduce the heat, simmer for 1¹/₂ hours or until tender. Drain and leave to cool thoroughly.

Chop the beans coarsely, then place in a bowl with the onion, tomatoes, sweetcorn, mango and coriander and toss well to combine.

For the dressing, place all the ingredients in a bowl except for the limes, pour over the bean salad and leave for 1 hour.

Cut the avocados in half lengthways and remove the stones. Peel them into long thin slices using a wide-bladed, swivel-headed peeler. Work quickly as they will go brown if left too long exposed to the air. You will need twenty slices in total. Chop any remaining avocado and add to the bean salad. Lay out the avocado slices on a flat surface, fill each with the salad mix and roll up tightly into neat rolls. Preheat a grill to its highest setting. Place the lime halves under the grill for 3–4 minutes until hot (this makes it easier to squeeze out the juice). Place five rolls per serving on a plate and garnish with rocket leaves. Squeeze the limes over the little rolls and serve immediately.

Aubergine kibbeh
with vegetable vinaigrette

Bulghur wheat has a distinctive nutty flavour, due to the inner layers of bran, which marries well with aubergine.

150ml olive oil

1 aubergine, cut into 1cm dice

1 onion, finely chopped

1 garlic clove, crushed

1 teaspoon smoked paprika

1/2 teaspoon ground cumin

120g bulghur (cracked wheat), cooked

juice of 1 lemon

1 beef tomato, blanched, peeled and quartered

fresh coriander leaves

salt and freshly ground black pepper

for the vegetable vinaigrette

1/2 roasted red pepper, peeled and diced

1/2 roasted green pepper, peeled and diced

2 teaspoons superfine capers

1 tablespoon chopped fresh coriander

3 tablespoons chopped fresh mint

2 tablespoons sherry vinegar

6 tablespoons olive oil

pinch of sugar

salt and freshly ground black pepper

for the mint yogurt

4 tablespoons natural yogurt

1 tablespoon chopped fresh mint

For the kibbeh, heat 100ml olive oil in a frying pan over a moderate heat. Add the aubergine and fry until golden. Add the onion, garlic, paprika and cumin and cook for a further 5–8 minutes. Add the cooked bulghur and sauté together for 2 minutes. Season to taste and leave to cool. Add the lemon juice and remaining oil.

For the vinaigrette, mix all the ingredients together in a bowl and season to taste. For the mint yogurt, mix the yogurt and mint together in a bowl.

Take a 5cm cutter and place on a serving plate. Fill with the kibbeh mixture. Using another 5cm cutter, cut out a circle from each quarter of tomato and place on the kibbeh and press down to compress the mixture. Prepare four servings in the same way and brush the tops with olive oil. Spoon the vinaigrette around each kibbeh and garnish with a spoonful of the mint yogurt. Serve chilled and garnish with coriander leaves.

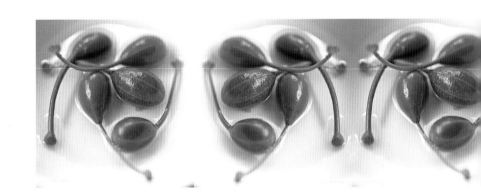

Aubergine and tomato rolls

with whipped pomegranate and chilli yogurt

This is my up-scale version of baba ghanoush, infused heartily with lots of bright fresh herbs and spices. Some flatbread makes a great accompaniment.

2 large aubergines

6 tablespoons olive oil

1 lemon, halved

4 garlic cloves, unpeeled

2 large green chillies, chopped

50g fresh mint leaves

100g fresh coriander leaves

1 teaspoon cumin seeds, dry-roasted

1 teaspoon cardamom seeds, dry-roasted

4 beef tomatoes, firm but juicy and ripe

aubergine crisps (see PG TIPS) – optional

8 lemon wedges

salt and freshly ground black pepper

for the pomegranate and chilli yogurt

1 teaspoon chilli oil

100ml thick natural yogurt

2 spring onions, finely chopped

1/2 garlic clove, crushed

1 fresh pomegranate, halved and seeds squeezed out

1 tablespoon chopped fresh mint

salt and freshly ground black pepper

Preheat the oven to 230°C/450°F/gas mark 8. Place the aubergines on a tinfoil-lined baking sheet, prick them all over with a sharp knife and drizzle with 5 tablespoons of olive oil. Place the lemon halves and garlic cloves alongside, put in the oven and roast for 25–30 minutes until the aubergines are very tender and charred all over. Remove and cool.

Place the green chillies, mint, coriander, dry-roasted spices and the remaining olive oil into a food processor and blend to a paste.

Halve the aubergines and carefully scoop out the inner flesh, leaving the skin. Place in a colander or muslin cloth and squeeze out the excess moisture. Add the flesh with the peeled roasted garlic to the spices in the food processor and blend to a smooth thick purée, scraping down the sides if necessary. Remove to a bowl, add the juices from the roasted lemon halves and season well to taste. Refrigerate until needed.

Using a kitchen mandolin or very sharp thin-bladed knife, cut the tomatoes into very thin slices. For each roll, lay out three rows of three overlapping slices of tomatoes on a small piece of clingfilm. Spoon on the chilled aubergine mixture and use the clingfilm to lift and fold each tomato roll into a roulade or cracker. Twist the ends and gently seal into a bonbon shape, then refrigerate for 30 minutes.

Meanwhile, fry the aubergine crisps (if using). For the pomegranate and chilli yogurt, whip the chilli oil and yogurt together, add the spring onions, garlic, pomegranate seeds and mint and season to taste.

Carefully unroll the clingfilm from the tomato rolls and gently place one on each serving plate, garnish with the aubergine crisps, lemon wedges and a good dollop of the yogurt. Serve immediately.

PG TIPS For the aubergine crisps, thinly slice 1 aubergine into 2mm thick slices, using a kitchen mandolin or thin-bladed knife. Lay on a tray and lightly season with salt to extract the excess water and leave for 30 minutes. Rinse lightly and dry well. Deep-fry them in hot vegetable oil at 170°C/325°F until golden and crisp. Remove onto kitchen paper to drain off any excess fat and keep at room temperature until ready for use.

Tuscan tomato bread pudding
with peas and broad beans

These individual little savoury bread puddings are delicious on their own, but when paired with the delicate-tasting spring peas and beans, bound in a little sauce made from their natural juices, it takes it straight to heaven! Shop-bought sunblush tomatoes may be used instead of your own oven-dried tomatoes if you wish.

100ml full-fat milk

300ml double cream

2 sprigs of fresh rosemary

2 free-range eggs

1 free-range egg yolk

50g ricotta cheese

2 crusty bread rolls, cut into 1cm slices

1 tablespoon extra-virgin olive oil

4 slices of mild goat's cheese

100g oven-dried tomatoes (see PG TIPS), chopped

2 tablespoons pesto sauce (see PG TIPS page 103)

salt, freshly ground black pepper and ground nutmeg

for the vegetables

180g fresh broad beans, shelled

100g fresh peas, shelled

100ml good vegetable stock

50g fresh tarragon leaves, chopped

1 shallot, finely chopped

20g unsalted butter, chilled and diced

2 tablespoons extra-virgin olive oil

4 x 125ml ramekins

Preheat the oven to 180°C/350°F/gas mark 4. Place the milk, cream and rosemary in a small pan, bring to the boil and simmer for 2–3 minutes. Remove from the heat, leave unstrained to infuse and cool. Strain through a fine strainer.

In a bowl, whisk together the eggs and egg yolk and gradually pour into the cream; season to taste with salt, pepper and nutmeg. Add the ricotta and mix well.

Butter four ramekins and place them in a roasting tin. Brush the bread slices with olive oil and arrange in the bases of the ramekins. Place the slices of goat's cheese on top and scatter over the oven-dried tomatoes. Gently pour over the prepared cream and fill to the top. Don't worry if the bread floats to the surface. Place the ramekins in a roasting tin and pour boiling water in the tin so it reaches halfway up the sides of the ramekins. Place in the oven for 30–40 minutes until cooked, then remove the dishes from the roasting tin. Keep them warm while you prepare the vegetables.

Blanch the broad beans in boiling water for 2 minutes, remove with a slotted spoon into iced water and then peel them. Cook the peas for 2–3 minutes and drain well. Heat the vegetable stock with 30g chopped tarragon and the shallot and leave to simmer for 1 minute. Place half the broad beans in a food processor with the tarragon stock and blend to a smooth creamy purée. Place the purée in a pan with the remaining beans and cooked peas and warm over a low heat. Add the butter, a little at a time, season to taste and add the remaining chopped tarragon and olive oil.

Turn out the tomato puddings onto serving plates, drizzle a little of the pesto over each bread topping. Spoon the peas and beans around the puddings and garnish with a sprig of rosemary, if desired. Serve immediately.

PG TIPS   For the oven-dried tomatoes, take 1kg blanched, peeled and deseeded plum tomatoes, then halve them lengthways. Arrange the tomatoes side by side on a baking dish, sprinkle lightly with sea salt and sugar, then scatter over some fresh thyme leaves. Drizzle with olive oil, place in a preheated oven, set at its lowest setting. Cook for about 1 hour, until very soft, then turn the tomatoes over, baste with their juices and cook for a further 1 hour, by which time they should be tender and shriveled to half the size. Cover with a little olive oil and refrigerate until needed.

Vegetable carpaccio
with saffron verde dressing – RAW

A vibrant and tasty raw vegetable appetiser from Piedmont in Italy. Its
success is reliant on the superb quality of the raw vegetables used, sliced
as thinly as possible and prepared just before serving.

for the dressing

1 garlic clove, crushed

100g fresh flat-leaf parsley

$^1/_2$ teaspoon red chilli, finely chopped

100ml extra-virgin olive oil

$^1/_2$ teaspoon powdered saffron

$^1/_2$ teaspoon Dijon mustard

15g fresh white breadcrumbs

1 teaspoon balsamic vinegar

1 tablespoon white wine vinegar

salt and freshly ground black pepper

2 small beetroots, trimmed and peeled

1 large head of fennel, peeled

2 sticks of celery, peeled

1 small cauliflower, florets only

4 red radishes

1 large courgette

1 small avocado, halved and stoned

For the dressing, place the garlic, parsley, chilli and oil in a blender or food processor
and blend to a coarse pulp. Add the saffron and mustard. Soak the breadcrumbs with
the vinegars for 1 minute, then add to the oil. Blend again briefly and season to taste.

Using a sharp knife or better still a kitchen mandolin, slice all the vegetables into
thin shavings. Cut the avocado into thin slices. Arrange the vegetables attractively, with
an eye for colour, on four serving plates, drizzle over the dressing and serve with lots
of country-style bread.

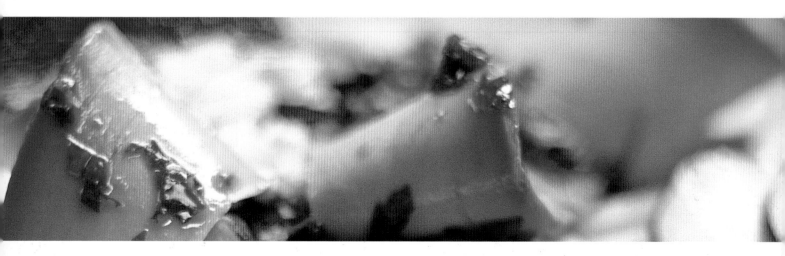

Beetroot caponata

One of the greatest dishes for me in the Italian repertoire is caponata, a type of sweet and sour relish. It's best made up to two days in advance to allow the flavours to develop. Traditionally made with aubergine and celery, my variation uses roast beetroot delicately flavoured with fresh basil and mint. This dish is great served with lots of crusty bread; sometimes I like to top it with grilled goat's cheese.

2 large raw beetroots
4 tablespoons extra-virgin olive oil
1 red onion, chopped
2 sticks of celery, stringed, cut into 1cm dice
2 tablespoons raisins
12 green olives, stoned
2 tablespoons superfine capers, rinsed and drained
3 tablespoons red wine vinegar
1 tablespoon balsamic vinegar
2 tablespoons brown sugar
2 tablespoons pine nuts, toasted
1 tablespoon chopped fresh purple basil
   (or green basil)
1 tablespoon chopped fresh mint

Preheat the oven to 180°C/350°F/gas mark 4. Wash the beetroots, drizzle with half the olive oil and wrap them in tinfoil. Place on a baking sheet and cook in the oven for up to 1 1/2 hours or until tender. Remove and cool before carefully peeling off their skins. Cut the beetroot into 1cm dice.

Heat the remaining oil in a large frying pan, add the onion and cook over a low heat until just softened. Add the celery and raisins and cook for a further 1 minute. Add the beetroot, olives and capers and mix well. Pour over the vinegars, add the sugar and raise the heat. Cook for 5–6 minutes until the syrup around the beetroot becomes sticky and jam-like in consistency. Add the pine nuts and herbs. Leave to cool to room temperature, then store in the fridge for up to 2 days before serving.

On the day, allow the caponata to come to room temperature before serving.

Baby shallots roasted in marsala
with peppers and basil

Shallots benefit from slow-roasting in an oven – they soften and release their natural sweetness during the process.

2 tablespoons vegetable or sunflower oil

400g medium-sized shallots, peeled, with root intact

pinch of ground cardamom

salt

1 tablespoon soft brown sugar

2 tablespoons balsamic vinegar

200ml marsala wine

4 red peppers

8 sun-dried tomatoes in oil, chopped

12 small basil leaves

Heat the oven to 200°C/400°F/gas mark 6. Heat the oil in a roasting tin on the hob large enough for the shallots and sauté them over a moderate heat until golden. Season with the ground cardamom, salt and sprinkle over the sugar. Lightly caramelise the shallots for 2–3 minutes, then pour over the vinegar, marsala and 100ml water. Bring to the boil, then transfer, uncovered, to the oven. Roast the shallots for 20–25 minutes, shaking the tin from time to time and basting them with the pan juices until they are soft, well coloured and glazed beautifully.

Meanwhile place the peppers in another roasting tin and cook for 20–25 minutes until the skins are blackened. Transfer to a bowl and cover with clingfilm for 5 minutes to loosen their skins. Skin, halve and deseed the peppers, then cut into wide strips. Place them on four plates, scatter over the tomatoes and drizzle over some of their preserving oil. Top with the warm shallots, scatter over the basil leaves and serve.

Zaatar crushed labna
with parsley, mint and olive oil

Zaatar is a dry spice and seed mixture popular throughout the Middle East. It is composed of dried thyme, sumac (a lemon-tasting red berry that is dried) and sesame seeds. It is purchased in its made-up form.

20 small labna cheese balls, drained and dried

3 tablespoons zaatar spice mix

2 plum tomatoes, cut into small dice

1 shallot, finely chopped

25g fresh mint leaves, chopped

25g fresh flat-leaf parsley, chopped

100ml mild olive oil

Middle Eastern style flatbread

Place the labna balls in a bowl, sprinkle over the zaatar and toss lightly to ensure an even coating. Set aside for 1 hour. Using a fork, lightly crush the cheese. Add the tomatoes, shallot and herbs and toss together again. Place on to serving plates in a pile, drizzle over the olive oil and serve with warmed flatbread.

Grilled portobello mushroooms

with mozzarella 'en carrozza' and pistachio pesto

If buffalo mozzarella is not available use cow's milk mozzarella. Panko crumbs are freeze-dried, which means they prevent the oil from soaking into the crumbs during frying. They can be sourced from oriental stores. Of course ordinary breadcrumbs could be used.

for the tomato vinaigrette

120g ripe tomatoes, chopped

2 tablespoons red wine vinegar

2 tablespoons tomato ketchup

1 teaspoon tomato purée

4 tablespoons extra-virgin olive oil

for the pistachio pesto

20 fresh basil leaves

25g pine nuts

30g pistachio nuts

3 garlic cloves, crushed

150ml extra-virgin olive oil

1 tablespoon freshly grated castelli vegetalia
   (parmesan-style cheese)

4 medium portobello mushrooms,

60ml extra-virgin olive oil

1 teaspoon fresh oregano

4 x 1cm thick slices buffalo mozzarella

plain flour for coating

2 free-range eggs, beaten

120g Japanese breadcrumbs (panko)

4 beef tomatoes, blanched, peeled and cut into
   1cm thick slices

salt and freshly ground black pepper

For the tomato vinaigrette, place all the ingredients in a small food processor and blend for 30 seconds. Strain through a fine strainer and refrigerate until needed.

For the pesto, put all the ingredients in a blender and blitz to a coarse paste. Set aside.

Slice each mushroom cap horizontally. Brush with a little olive oil on both sides of each slice and place on a baking tray, cut-side up. Season well.

Sprinkle oregano and a little seasoning over the mozzarella and carefully dredge the pieces in flour, then into beaten egg and finally through the breadcrumbs.

Heat a ridged grill pan, brush with a little olive oil and grill the mushrooms for 3–4 minutes until golden and lightly charred all over.

Meanwhile heat the remaining oil in a large frying pan, add the mozzarella slices and cook for 2–3 minutes on each side until golden. Remove and drain on kitchen paper. Place four mushroom bases on individual plates, put a well seasoned slice of tomato on top and then a slice of fried mozzarella. Place the mushroom lids on the top to reform the original shape. Add a good spoonful of the pistachio pesto and drizzle some tomato vinaigrette around the plate to serve.

Soups

Why is it that soup is so often considered to be an unadventurous and safe option for serving as an appetiser? Of course this is not how soups should be or need be! Soups are one of the most satisfying of foods, whether served chilled in the height of summer or hot to ward off the cold in winter months. The secret of any well prepared soup is the inclusion of an excellent basic stock.

Spelt soup
with Jerusalem artichokes and saffron

In Britain modern cooks are rediscovering the full flavour of whole grains like spelt, and not before time. They have long been popular in Europe, especially Italy, where spelt is more commonly known as farro and is used in all manner of tasty dishes. It is very nutritious and the perfect answer for those people who want to eat good, hearty grain products. It is available from health food shops.

150g fine spelt (preferably organic)

50g unsalted butter

1 onion, chopped

1 garlic clove, crushed

300g Jerusalem artichokes, well scrubbed and
  thinly sliced

6 fresh sage leaves

pinch of saffron

750ml good vegetable stock, hot

150ml single cream

40g pecorino cheese (ewe's milk cheese)

1 tablespoon extra-virgin olive oil

salt and freshly cracked black pepper

Soak the spelt overnight in a bowl of cold water and drain.

Melt the butter in a pan, add the onion and garlic and cook for 3–4 minutes until slightly softened. Add the artichokes, sage and saffron and mix well. Pour in the hot vegetable stock and bring to the boil. Add the spelt, cover and simmer gently for 20–25 minutes or until the artichokes are tender. (Reserve 25g cooked spelt for the garnish.) Transfer to a food processor and blend until smooth, then return the soup to a clean pan. Add the cream and return to the boil; season with salt and freshly cracked black pepper.

Meanwhile, grate the pecorino cheese as fine as possible and mix it with the reserved spelt in a bowl. Divide the soup between four serving bowls, sprinkle over the spelt and pecorino mixture and drizzle over the olive oil. Serve immediately.

Mushroom tom yum

This soup has its origins firmly rooted in the southern Asian region of Thailand. Classic Tom Yum soup contains fish or meat, but this variation using wild mushrooms lacks nothing less than the former. Galangal is a type of camphorised ginger root available from Thai stores, although root ginger could be used instead. The use of shiitake mushrooms adds a meaty flavour to the broth.

900ml good vegetable stock

4cm piece of galangal, peeled, cut into thin slices

2 sticks of lemongrass, outer casing discarded, thinly shredded

1 tablespoon vegetarian fish sauce (nuoc mam chay)

3 kaffir lime leaves, torn into small pieces

275g wild mushrooms of your choice (including shiitake, or use all shiitake)

2 teaspoons red Thai curry paste

2 large shallots, thinly sliced

3 tomatoes, cut into 1cm dice

juice of 2 limes

little coarse sea salt

40g fresh coriander leaves

Bring the vegetable stock to the boil, add the galangal and lemongrass and cook for 3–4 minutes. Add the fish sauce, lime leaves and mushrooms and simmer for 5 minutes. Stir in the curry paste. Add the shallots and diced tomatoes and cook for a further 2 minutes. Finish with the lime juice and a little salt. Taste the soup – it should be spicy, sour and a little salty. Pour into individual soup bowls and scatter over the coriander leaves.

Spiced carrot soup

with crispy egg noodles and Vietnamese mint

In this Asian soup (Tom Kha), coconut milk adds a wonderful sweet creaminess while the mint adds a refreshing fragrance. Egg noodles can be purchased from leading stores or oriental grocers. Vietnamese mint or 'hot' mint is in fact not a mint at all. Revered in the Far East, it has a slightly spicy, acidic flavour. It's worth shopping around for but normal mint is fine if it's not available.

vegetable oil for deep-frying

100g egg noodles

25g unsalted butter

2 garlic cloves, crushed

1 teaspoon Thai yellow curry paste

400g carrots, peeled and cut into 1cm dice

1 onion, chopped

2 sticks of lemongrass, outer casing discarded,
  finely shredded

2cm piece of root ginger, peeled and thinly shredded

700ml good vegetable stock

juice of 1/2 lime

10 leaves Vietnamese mint, torn

200ml coconut milk

2 spring onions, finely chopped

8 lime wedges

Heat the vegetable oil in a large pan or fryer. When the temperature is about 160°C/325°F add the noodles and fry for about 1 minute until crisp. Remove with a slotted spoon and drain on kitchen paper. Set aside.

Heat the butter in a pan, add the garlic and curry paste and cook together for 30 seconds. Add the diced carrot, onion, lemongrass and ginger and cook for 2–3 minutes. Pour in the vegetable stock, add the lime juice and bring to the boil. Reduce the heat and simmer for 10–15 minutes. Add the mint and coconut milk and cook for a further 1 minute.

Serve in individual soup bowls and top with a small nest of the crispy egg noodles. Scatter over the spring onions and serve with the lime wedges for your guests to squeeze over the soup.

Cajun black bean soup
with smoked tomato nachos

For a chunkier version of this soup, leave the beans whole. To quick-soak
the beans, cover them in cold water, bring to the boil and cook, uncovered,
over a moderate heat for 2 minutes. Leave to soak, covered, for 1 hour.

¹/2 teaspoon black peppercorns

¹/2 teaspoon coriander seeds

¹/2 teaspoon cumin seeds

1 small bay leaf

¹/2 teaspoon cayenne pepper

25g fresh oregano, chopped

10g fresh thyme, picked

50g unsalted butter

1 onion, chopped

1 stick of celery, chopped

2 garlic cloves, crushed

375g drained black beans, soaked overnight

juice of ¹/2 lemon

salt

for the nachos

2 tablespoons olive oil

1 shallot, finely chopped

1 small garlic clove, crushed

¹/2 teaspoon smoked paprika

600g sunblush tomatoes

1 tablespoon chopped fresh coriander leaves

2 corn tortillas, each cut into 8 wedges

vegetable oil for deep-frying

40g grated vegetarian cheddar cheese

little sour cream (optional)

salt and freshly ground black pepper

Grind the peppercorns, seeds and bay leaf in a mortar or spice grinder, add the
cayenne, oregano and thyme and mix well. Heat the butter in a medium-sized pan,
add the onion, celery and garlic and cook for 2–3 minutes. Add the ground spices
and cook for a further 3–4 minutes. Add the soaked beans and 1.5 litres water and
bring to the boil. Reduce the heat and simmer for 1¹/2–2 hours or until the beans
are tender. Transfer to a food processor and blend until smooth. Adjust the seasoning
and add the lemon juice. Set aside.

For the nachos, heat the olive oil in a pan, add the shallot, garlic, smoked paprika
and sunblush tomatoes and cook for 4–5 minutes until softened. Add the chopped
coriander and season to taste. Deep-fry the tortilla wedges until crisp in hot oil and
then drain on kitchen paper. Top with the tomato mixture and sprinkle over the
grated cheese. Place the tortillas under a hot preheated grill until the cheese melts.
Meanwhile reheat the soup and then pour into serving bowls and top with 1–2
tomato nachos. Serve with sour cream, if desired.

Fennel soup
with star anise, hazelnuts and tarragon

This soup is very elegant; in the summer months it is delicious served cold.

50g unsalted butter

1 onion, thinly sliced

2 heads of fennel, fronds removed and reserved, thinly sliced

175g potatoes, cut into small pieces

600ml milk

60g hazelnuts, crushed

3 star anise

120ml whipping cream

2 tablespoons chopped fresh tarragon

1 tablespoon anise liquor (eg. Pernod or Ricard)

salt and freshly ground black pepper

Heat the butter in a pan, add the onion and fennel and cook for about 12–15 minutes, until softened. Add the potatoes, milk, 600ml water and hazelnuts and bring to the boil. Add the star anise and simmer for 25 minutes or until all the vegetables are very soft. Remove the star anise and transfer the mixture to a food processor. Blend until very smooth. Return to a clean pan, add the cream, chopped tarragon and anise liquor and return to the boil.

Blitz with a hand-held blender until light and frothy and season to taste. Pour into serving bowls, scatter over the reserved fennel fronds and serve.

English pea and mint soup
with truffle ricotta foam

By quickly cooking the vegetables, they retain their colour and natural taste.

400g fresh or frozen peas

20g fresh mint leaves

1 onion, chopped

1 leek, chopped

750ml good vegetable stock

270ml skimmed milk

1 tablespoon extra-virgin olive oil

20g unsalted butter

1 teaspoon truffle oil

15g unsalted butter

2 tablespoons ricotta cheese

salt and freshly cracked black pepper

Bring a large pan of boiling salted water to the boil. Add the peas, mint leaves, onion and leek and simmer gently for about 5–6 minutes until tender. Drain them in a colander, then refresh under cold running water. When they are fully drained, transfer to a food processor and blend to a smooth purée, scraping down the sides once or twice to ensure all the purée is satiny smooth.

Place the vegetable stock and 150ml milk in a pan, add the purée, olive oil and butter and bring to the boil, whisking frequently. Season with salt and freshly cracked black pepper.

In another pan, bring the remaining 120ml milk, truffle oil and butter to the boil. Add the ricotta and blitz with a hand-held blender until smooth and frothy. Divide the soup between four bowls, then spoon over the ricotta foam to serve.

Fruit ceviche soup
with Thai basil oil – RAW

This welcoming summer soup is an adaptation of one of my old recipes, but in this version the fruits take on more definition and texture, while the drizzle of Thai basil oil adds that magical taste of fragrant aniseed.

for the oil

50g Thai basil (holy basil)

75ml groundnut or vegetable oil

for the soup

200g fresh pineapple, diced

1 ripe mango, diced

1.5cm piece of root ginger, peeled and finely grated

1 tablespoon tamarind paste

2 tablespoons maple syrup

300ml fresh orange juice

freshly cracked black pepper

for the fruit ceviche

75g fresh pineapple, cut into 5mm dice

1/2 mango, cut into 5mm dice

small wedge of orange

fresh melon (charentais or cantaloupe) cut into 5mm dice

1 small red onion, finely chopped

2 kiwis, cut into 5mm dice

1 pasilla chilli, deseeded, finely chopped

juice of 2 limes, zest of 1

For the oil, place the basil and oil in a blender and blitz to a purée, then strain it and refrigerate, covered, until needed.

For the soup, place the pineapple, mango and ginger in a bowl and leave to marinate at room temperature for 1 hour.

Meanwhile for the ceviche, place all the ingredients in a bowl and toss well together. Set aside.

Place the marinated fruits and ginger in a food processor and add the tamarind paste, maple syrup and orange juice. Blend to a fine purée and then strain or sieve into a bowl. Chill for a good 2–3 hours.

Place the ceviche into the centre of four well-chilled shallow soup bowls, pour over the soup, crack over some fresh black pepper and drizzle Thai basil oil over. Serve immediately.

Cool cucumber soup
with Indian spices

Another great summer soup. Being a lover of all foods from the Far East, this soup makes a regular appearance on my menus. It is light and delicately spiced and really gets the gastric juices going. If you are serving the naan bread, I recommend it served hot – it makes a good contrast.

for the curry paste

2 tablespoons mild curry powder

1 tablespoon garam masala

1/2 teaspoon mustard seeds

1 teaspoon cumin seeds

2 teaspoons prepared curry paste

1 garlic clove, crushed

for the cucumber soup

2 cucumbers, peeled and halved lengthways

1 small red chilli, halved, seeds removed and finely chopped ·

700ml thick natural yogurt

2 tablespoons chopped fresh mint leaves

little lemon juice

salt and freshly ground black pepper

hot naan bread, cut into fingers (optional)

For the curry paste, mix the curry powder and garam masala in a bowl. Add 3 tablespoons of water and mix to a paste. Set aside.

Heat a frying pan over a moderate heat, throw in the mustard and cumin seeds and dry-fry them for 20–30 seconds until they give off an aromatic fragrance. Add the curry paste and garlic, reduce the heat to very low and cook for 1 minute. Remove and leave to cool.

For the cucumber soup, remove the seeds from the cucumbers and cut them into chunks. Place them in a food processor, add the chilli and curry paste and blend to a fairly smooth liquid. Strain through a sieve. Pour into a bowl, whisk in the yogurt, add the mint and a squeeze of lemon juice to taste; season. Refrigerate until needed. Serve in four soup bowls with the naan bread, if using.

Potato cream soup
with wild mushrooooms and soft-boiled egg

New potatoes and wild mushrooms combine to make a delicate soup.

50g unsalted butter

1 onion, chopped

1 large leek, sliced

300g large new potatoes, peeled and halved

750ml good vegetable stock, hot

100ml whole milk

4 free-range eggs

145g dried wild mushrooms, soaked in warm water for
*   30 minutes*

coarse sea salt and freshly cracked black pepper

Heat half the butter in a pan, add the onion and leek and cook over a low heat for 4–5 minutes until softened. Add the potatoes and cook for a further 1 minute. Pour over the stock, reduce the heat and simmer for 20 minutes or until the potatoes are soft. Transfer to a food processor, add the milk and remaining butter and blend until smooth in texture.

Bring a pan of water to the boil, reduce the heat, add the eggs and simmer for 4 minutes. Remove the eggs with a slotted spoon and immerse into a bowl of cold water, before shelling them carefully, keeping them intact. Return the soup to a clean pan, add the soaked wild mushrooms and soaking liquid, cook for 1 minute and adjust the seasoning to taste. Place a soft-boiled egg into each serving bowl, pour over the hot soup carefully and sprinkle the egg with seasoning and serve.

Buttermilk sweetcorn bisque
with radish and wild garlic

This is a chilled variation of chowder made with buttermilk.

20g unsalted butter

1 onion, chopped

1 stick of celery, chopped

2 garlic cloves, crushed

sprig of fresh thyme

3 corn on the cob, kernels detached, cob centres reserved

300ml single cream

100ml buttermilk

4 small red radishes

1 small bunch of wild garlic leaves (or chives)

salt, freshly ground black pepper and a pinch of
*   cayenne pepper*

Melt the butter in a large pan, add the onion, celery, garlic and thyme and leave to cook over a low heat for 10–12 minutes until the vegetables are soft. Add 750ml water to the vegetables with the cob centres. Bring to the boil, reduce the heat and simmer for 20 minutes over a gentle heat until the liquid becomes flavourful. Remove the cob centres and discard. Add the sweetcorn kernels and cream to the liquid and simmer for 10 minutes. Remove half of the kernels for garnishing and leave to cool.

Transfer the cooled soup to a food processor and blend until smooth. Strain it and then refrigerate until needed. To serve, add the buttermilk, season with salt, pepper and pinch of cayenne and add the reserved kernels to the soup. Pour into four individual soup bowls. Garnish with a little pile of grated or shredded red radish and some shredded wild garlic leaves. Serve well chilled.

Beetroot gazpacho

with apple and frozen avocado cream

A real treat for a hot summer's day, this chilled beetroot soup is
delicately lifted with a little horseradish; try it as it will soon become a
summer favourite.

1kg ripe plum tomatoes, cut into small chunks

1 small onion, chopped

1 small green pepper, deseeded, cut into small chunks

1 garlic clove, crushed

1 slice of stale bread

5 tablespoons extra-virgin olive oil

3 tablespoons good-quality sherry vinegar

1 tablespoon creamed horseradish

*2 roasted beetroot, peeled and chopped (see
  page 46)*

1 Granny Smith apple

salt and freshly ground black pepper

frozen avocado cream (see page 78)

Place the tomatoes, onion, pepper, garlic and bread in a food processor and blend to
a fine purée. With the motor running, gently pour in a thin stream of the oil through
the funnel at the top and blend until it thickens and forms an emulsion. Add the
vinegar, horseradish and beetroot, then blend again until smooth; season to taste.
(If you prefer a smoother soup, pass it through a fine strainer too.) The flavour should
be slightly sweet and sour – add a little more vinegar if necessary. Chill for 4 hours
or overnight.

Pour the chilled soup into four shallow soup bowls. Peel the apple, remove the
centre core, then shred into fine strips using a kitchen mandolin or with a sharp knife.
Place a ball of avocado cream in the centre of each soup and sprinkle over the finely
shredded apple.

Puy lentil bouillabaisse
with wilted spinach, fennel and saffron rouille

The king of lentils – the puy lentil – is best for this earthy rustic-style
soup; they taste wonderful and hold their shape well during cooking.

for the rouille

1 medium-sized potato

1 small garlic clove, crushed

1 small red pepper, roasted and peeled

1 free-range egg yolk

pinch of good quality saffron (or powdered)

3 tablespoons extra-virgin olive oil

*salt, freshly ground black pepper and pinch of
    cayenne pepper*

2 tablespoons olive oil

1 onion, chopped

2 garlic cloves, crushed

*pinch of good-quality saffron (or 1/2 teaspoon
    powdered saffron)*

1 small head of fennel, cut into 1/2cm dice

1/2 teaspoon fennel seeds

175g puy lentils

1/2 teaspoon mild paprika

1 litre good vegetable stock

100g baby spinach leaves

4 slices of country-style bread, cut into 1cm cubes

For the rouille, cook the potato in its skin in a pan of boiling water (or alternatively bake in the oven), remove and, when cool enough to handle, peel off the skin. Place the garlic and pepper in a blender and blitz to a purée. Add the cooked potato, egg yolk, saffron, salt, pepper and a good pinch of cayenne pepper. With the motor running, gently pour in a thin stream of oil through the funnel at the top, as if making mayonnaise, until it thickens and forms an emulsion.

Heat 1 tablespoon of olive oil in a pan, add the onion, garlic, saffron, fennel and fennel seeds and cook for 4–5 minutes until tender. Add the puy lentils, mild paprika and stock and bring to the boil. Cook rapidly for 2–3 minutes, then reduce the heat and simmer for 30 minutes or until the lentils are just cooked. Stir in the spinach and allow to wilt in the soup.

Toast the bread cubes (or fry them in a little olive oil) and place in four serving bowls. Pour over the soup and drizzle over 1 tablespoon of olive oil. Serve the saffron rouille alongside for the guests to stir into the soup themselves. Serve hot.

Chilled avocado

and almond milk guacomole – RAW

A delightfully simple soup of Mexican origin, which needs no cooking for those of you who are raw food enthusiasts. The soup should be made just before serving, but if you do plan to make it and keep it for several hours, lay clingfilm over the surface of the bowl – this will stop the surface of the soup from discolouring and darkening if stored for longer than 1 hour.

2 ripe but not too ripe avocados, cold (preferably
  Haas variety)
1 onion, finely chopped
1 garlic clove, crushed
2 green chillies, deseeded and finely chopped
40g fresh coriander leaves
2 tomatoes, cut into small pieces
300ml almond milk (see PG TIPS)
2–3 tablespoons lime juice
salt and freshly ground black pepper

100ml sour cream or crème fraîche
1/2 avocado, cut into cubes
1 teaspoon lime zest
1 tablespoon fresh coriander leaves

Halve the avocados, remove the stones and scoop out the flesh into a food processor. Add the onion, garlic, chilli, coriander leaves, tomatoes and almond milk and blend for about 1 minute until smooth. Add 300ml water and enough lime juice to add balance to the soup and blend again. Season with salt and freshly ground black pepper. (If you prefer a smoother soup, pass it through a fine strainer too.) Place in a bowl and cover with clingfilm if storing for later. To serve immediately, pour into shallow soup bowls, top with a good dollop of sour cream, the diced avocado, lime zest and coriander leaves. Serve well chilled.

PG TIPS   Nut milks used in raw cooking provide richness and sweetness to a dish. To make almond milk, soak 300g almonds in 600ml pure still water (purified or bottled) and soak overnight at room temperature. Rinse the almonds under cold water and drain well. Place in a food processor and add 900ml purified water and blend until as smooth as possible. Strain through a fine strainer or cheesecloth and then refrigerate until needed.

Roasted pepper passata

with basil yogurt and tomato tartare

Roasting the tomatoes and peppers for this soup really adds depth of flavour to the end result. The addition of a basil-flavoured yogurt and a fresh-tasting tomato tartare complete a great soup.

for the passata

8 ripe plum tomatoes, halved

2 red peppers, halved, deseeded and chopped small

1 onion, quartered

2 garlic cloves, peeled

sprig of fresh thyme

2 tablespoons olive oil

900ml good vegetable stock, hot

1 tablespoon tomato purée

salt and freshly ground black pepper

for the basil yogurt

50g fresh basil leaves

40ml extra-virgin olive oil

4 tablespoons natural thick set yogurt

for the tomato tartare

2 plum tomatoes, blanched and seeded

1 small garlic clove, crushed

1 tablespoon maple syrup

juice of $^1/_2$ lime

1 tablespoon chopped fresh basil

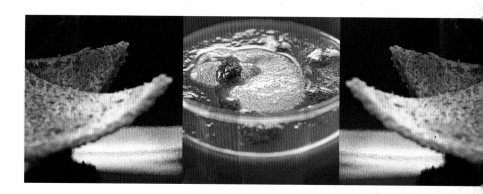

Preheat the oven to 220°C/425°F/gas mark 7. Place the tomatoes, peppers, onion, garlic and thyme in a roasting tin, spoon over the olive oil and season. Roast them for 20–25 mintues, until wilted and slightly charred all over (alternatively, this could be done under a hot grill). Transfer to a pan, pour over the stock and add the tomato purée. Cook over a moderate heat for 15 minutes. Strain the soup through a sieve or strainer and return it to a clean pan, adjust the seasoning and keep warm.

For the yogurt, blanch the basil leaves for 15 seconds in boiling water, then remove immediately with a slotted spoon into iced water. Dry the blanched leaves in a cloth. Place the leaves in a small blender with the olive oil and blitz until smooth. Break down the yogurt with a small whisk to a creamy texture and stir in the basil oil.

For the tomato tartare, mix all the ingredients in a bowl and season to taste. Reheat the soup to boiling point, then pour into four bowls. Place two good spoonfuls of yogurt in the centre of each bowl, followed by a good spoonful of basil on top. Place a little chilled tomato tartare to one side and serve immediately.

PG TIPS A nice accompaniment is crisp melba toasts. Toast slices of white or brown bread under a hot grill on both sides. Remove the crusts, halve horizontally and cut into triangles. Grill the untoasted sides for a few seconds until the edges curl. Set aside to cool.

Salads

I have always been fascinated by salads – long gone are the days when a simple lettuce mixed with tomato and cucumber sufficed. I have included designer-style salads for the beginner as well as the experienced cook. Vibrant, nutritious and varied, these salads can be eaten as appetisers, main courses or for any healthy lunch or supper. I hope they will introduce you to exciting new tastes and combinations from around the globe and act as an inspirational starting point for your own salad creations.

Jerusalem artichoke, bean and fennel salad

with green peppercorn ajo-blanco

A variation on a salad I recently enjoyed in Alicante in Spain. I've replaced globe artichokes with Jerusalem artichokes and created a peppery almond and garlic dressing to give the salad a pleasant lift. If artichokes are not available use new potatoes.

for the green peppercorn ajo-blanco

50g whole blanched almonds

25g pine nuts

2 garlic cloves, crushed

50g fresh white breadcrumbs

100ml iced water

4 tablespoons extra-virgin olive oil

2 tablespoons sherry vinegar

salt

2 free-range egg yolks

4 tablespoons double cream

1 teaspoon green peppercorns, rinsed and drained

16 Jerusalem artichokes

200g French beans, topped and tailed

1 large head of fennel, fronds removed

splash of sherry vinegar

2 tablespoons extra-virgin olive oil

1 large shallot, thinly sliced

50g flaked almonds, toasted

salt and freshly ground black pepper

For the ajo-blanco, place the almonds, pine nuts and garlic in a food processor and blend them as fine as possible, scraping down the sides of the machine if necessary. Do not over-process or the nuts will become oily. Add the breadcrumbs and a quarter of the iced water and blend again to a fine purée. With the motor running, gently pour in a thin stream of the oil and half the vinegar through the funnel at the top. When smooth, add the egg yolks and blitz again. Strain into a bowl, add salt and the remaining water and vinegar. Stir in the cream, add the peppercorns and refrigerate until required. Check the consistency before mixing with the vegetables – it should be the consistency of single cream – if it's too thick add a little more water.

Wash and peel the artichokes, cutting off the knobbly bits in order to obtain a cylindrical shape about 3cm in diameter. Cook them in lightly simmering salted water for 12–15 minutes, according to size. Drain and then slice them into 5cm thick pieces. Keep warm.

At the same time, cook the French beans for 5–6 minutes until just tender. Drain well and add to the artichokes.

Using a kitchen mandolin, thinly shave the fennel onto the artichokes and beans, add a splash of vinegar, the olive oil and shallot slices and season to taste. Add the dressing, toss carefully together and adjust the seasoning. Place in four salad bowls, garnished with the toasted almonds.

PG TIPS Jerusalem artichokes have a very soft texture when cooked, so it is important to watch them carefully as they cook – the water should not be allowed to boil rapidly or they will become mushy so check their texture regularly as they cook.

Roasted tomato, goat's cheese and asparagus salad
with basil purée and lavender oil

Summer is the time to enjoy this most fragrant of salads, made with
perfectly ripe tomatoes, ideally ripened on the vine. The basil purée and
lavender oil completes an air of Provence. I suggest serving this salad
with lots of fresh chunky baguette bread to mop up the juices.

for the basil purée

20g fresh basil leaves (plus some for garnishing)

1 small garlic clove, crushed

6 tablespoons extra-virgin olive oil

for the lavender oil

good sprig of fresh or dried lavender

6 tablespoons extra-virgin olive oil

for the salad

20 small (4cm) vine-ripened tomatoes

1 teaspoon caster sugar

1 teaspoon fresh thyme leaves

*4 mature goat's cheeses (or 2 logs), cut
  to make 20 thin slices*

8 asparagus tips, prepared

12 black olives, stoned

2 tablespoons extra-virgin olive oil

1 tablespoon red wine vinegar

1 tablespoon balsamic vinegar

salt and freshly ground black pepper

Preheat the oven to 180°C/350°F/gas mark 4. For the basil purée, place the basil
and garlic in a blender with the oil and blitz to a smooth purée. Transfer to a bowl.

For the lavender oil, remove the flowers from the lavender plant and place in a
bowl. Heat the oil in a pan and, when hot, pour in the flowers, remove from the heat
and leave to steep for 2 minutes, then strain off the oil. (Leaving to steep any longer
tends to make the oil bitter.)

For the salad, remove the tomatoes from their vine, then cut each in half
horizontally through the centre. Sprinkle the cut tomatoes with salt, pepper, a little
sugar and thyme. Place a slice of goat's cheese between the two halves of each
tomato, so that you have twenty reformed tomatoes stuffed with the cheese.

Place the asparagus and olives in a baking dish, pour over the olive oil and roast
in the oven for 6–8 minutes. Add the cheese-stuffed tomatoes to the baking dish,
drizzle over both vinegars and cook for a further 4–5 minutes or until the tomatoes
just begin to soften. Place the baked tomatoes on four serving plates, add the
asparagus and olives and drizzle over the basil purée and lavender oil.

Cumin-roasted squash salad
with peppers and chocolate dressing

Don't be put off by the sound of chocolate dressing for the salad. The flavours of the salad are representative of Latino cooking; you will be amazed just how delicate it can be. The combination of spices and chocolate has been used successfully for centuries in South America.

1 large butternut squash, peeled and cut into neat wedges
2 yellow peppers, halved and deseeded
$^1/_2$ teaspoon cumin seeds
3 tablespoons olive oil
1 red onion, thinly sliced
6 red radishes, thinly sliced
75g fresh coriander leaves
salt and freshly ground black pepper

for the chocolate dressing
100ml fresh orange juice
$^1/_2$ garlic clove, crushed
1 tablespoon white wine vinegar
1 tablespoon honey
$^1/_2$ teaspoon chilli powder
1 tablespoon lime juice
6 tablespoons olive oil
20g good-quality bitter chocolate (70% cocoa solids),
   melted and kept warm
salt and freshly ground black pepper

Preheat the oven to 180°C/350°F/gas mark 4. Place the squash and peppers in a large roasting tin. In a mortar, crush the cumin seeds with a pestle to a fine powder. Season the vegetables with the cumin and drizzle over the olive oil. Place in the oven to roast for 25–30 minutes until tender and slightly caramelised. Remove the peppers from the oven, peel, cut them into thick slices and return them to the squash. Turn off the oven and keep warm.

For the dressing, place the orange juice in a pan with the garlic, vinegar and honey and bring to the boil. Cook for 2 minutes to form a light syrup. Transfer to a bowl, whisk in the chilli powder, lime juice, olive oil and warm melted chocolate and season to taste. Place the roasted vegetables on four serving plates and scatter over the onion and radish. Pour over the dressing and garnish with the coriander leaves. Serve warm.

Red tofu salad
with beans, persimmon, mint and cashews

Although I'm not a great lover of tofu, I can appreciate the enjoyment and
nutritional aspects it can bring. This delicate marinade adds a sweet yet
hot coating to the tofu, topping a wonderfully fragrant and fresh salad.

250g pack firm tofu, drained

2 tablespoons plum sauce

2 tablespoons dark soy sauce

1 tablespoon honey

3 teaspoons sweet chilli sauce

2 tablespoons cashew nuts, roasted and roughly chopped

*2 persimmons (Sharon fruit), stem removed and cut
 into wedges*

325g French beans, topped and tailed

2 tablespoons groundnut or vegetable oil

salt and freshly ground black pepper

for the dressing

2 tablespoons palm sugar (or brown sugar)

2 tablespoons coarse sea salt

2 garlic cloves, chopped

good handful of mint leaves

4 hot green chillies, deseeded and chopped

1cm piece of root ginger, peeled and grated

3 tablespoons vegetarian fish sauce (nuoc mam chay)

juice of 8 limes

4 shallots, thinly sliced

Cut the tofu in half widthways, then cut both pieces in half horizontally to give four
equally thick slices. In a shallow dish combine the plum sauce, soy sauce, honey and
sweet chilli sauce. Place the tofu slices in the marinade and leave to marinate for
2 hours, turning them regularly to ensure the tofu is thoroughly coated. Cook the
beans in a pan of boiling salted water for 2–3 minutes or until just cooked, but still
retaining a good bite.

For the dressing, melt the palm sugar in a small pan. Place the salt, garlic and
mint in a mortar and lightly pound to a pulp with a pestle. Add the chillies, palm sugar
and ginger and pound again. Add the fish sauce, lime juice and shallots and mix well.
Leave for 1 hour for the flavours to develop. Place the cashews, persimmons and
beans in a bowl and pour over the prepared dressing. Toss well and season to taste.
Remove the tofu from the marinade. Heat a large frying pan with the oil, add the tofu
and cook for about 2 minutes on each side until golden and crisp. Place a good pile
of the salad on four serving plates, top each with 1–2 slices of tofu and serve at once.

Grilled baby aubergine salad

with roasted rice and coriander dressing

Vietnamese coriander can be found in Asian stores, although regular
coriander could be substituted.

4 tablespoons sunflower oil

8 baby aubergines

for the dressing

juice of 4 limes, zest of 1

1 tablespoon palm sugar (or brown sugar)

1 small green chilli

2 teaspoons kecap manis (Indonesian soy sauce)

2 teaspoons dry-roasted basmati rice (see PG TIPS)

2 banana shallots, peeled and thinly sliced

100g fresh Vietnamese coriander leaves

50g fresh mint leaves

salt and freshly ground black pepper

Heat a ridged grill pan over a high heat and brush with the oil. Cut the aubergines in half lengthways, place on the grill and cook for about 6–8 minutes, turning them regularly, until golden and lightly charred all over.

For the dressing, place the zest and juice of the limes, the palm sugar, chilli and soy sauce in a bowl and stir until the sugar has dissolved. Add the roasted rice, sliced shallots, coriander and mint leaves, season to taste and mix well.

Place the grilled aubergines on a large serving platter, spoon over the dressing and serve immediately.

PG TIPS   To prepare Asian-style roasted rice, heat the oven to 180°C/350°F/gas mark 4. Place 10g basmati rice in a baking tray and put in the oven to dry-roast for 20–25 minutes until golden. Remove and cool. Place in a mortar and crush with the pestle to a coarse powder. Keep in a sealed jar ready for use.

Broad bean crostini salad

with black olive oil and iced goat's cheese

The new microplane-style graters are fantastic for shaving the iced goat's cheese at the last minute for this dish. They are now readily available in most good cookery shops. Try to source a mature goat's cheese for this recipe – it will really repay your efforts.

1 firm, mature goat's cheese

50g black olives, stoned

1/2 garlic clove, crushed

100ml extra-virgin olive oil

750g fresh broad beans, shelled

100g young rocket leaves

12 fresh tarragon leaves

1 tablespoon sherry vinegar

1 ciabatta loaf, cut into 8 x 1cm thick slices

salt and freshly ground black pepper

Wrap the goat's cheese in a little parcel of tinfoil and place in the freezer for up to 2 hours until hard.

Place the black olives, half the garlic and 75ml olive oil in a blender and blitz until coarsely chopped. Set aside.

Cook the broad beans in boiling salted water for 4–5 minutes and then drain. Using thumbs and forefinger push out the inner beans from the tough outer skin.

Heat the remaining oil in a non-stick frying pan, add the remaining garlic, the rocket, broad beans and tarragon and cook together for 1 minute until the rocket begins to wilt. Add the vinegar, toss together and season.

Lightly toast the ciabatta slices on both sides under the grill and then smear one side with black olive oil. Dress each slice with the wilted rocket and bean mix and place on four serving plates. Remove the cheese from the freezer and, using a small grater, finely grate the iced cheese all over the top of each crostini.
Serve immediately.

PG TIPS   I often vary this dish using artichokes instead of broad beans. A little trickle of truffle oil makes a wonderful addition.

Salad of palm hearts, beetroot and asparagus

with pomegranate dressing

Pomegranates are, I admit, one of the most challenging of fruits for any cook, but with a little patience in their preparation, they make a wonderful, colourful addition to salads. Palm hearts can be purchased from good delicatessens and supermarkets.

2 medium-sized beetroots

2 tablespoons olive oil

16 asparagus tips, trimmed

4 palm hearts (tinned), sliced lengthways

2 red chicory, leaves separated

100g watercress, stems removed

10 fresh basil leaves

2 tablespoons pistachio nuts, roughly chopped

for the pomegranate dressing

150ml fresh orange juice

1 tablespoon fresh lemon juice

1 tablespoon white wine vinegar

2 tablespoons mild olive oil

1 tablespoon vegetable oil

1 fresh pomegranate

salt and freshly ground black pepper

Preheat the oven to 180°C/350°F/gas mark 4. Wash the beetroots, drizzle with olive oil and wrap them in tinfoil. Place on a baking tray and bake in the oven for 1 hour or until just tender. Remove and cool slightly before peeling and then cut each one into ten wedges. Cook the asparagus in boiling salted water for 1 minute, drain and then refresh in cold water.

For the dressing, place the orange juice and lemon juice in a small pan and cook over a moderate heat until the liquid has reduced by half and become slightly syrupy. Pour into a bowl and leave to cool. When cool, stir in the vinegar and whisk in both oils. Cut the pomegranate in half horizontally and then squeeze out the fruit in the palm of your hand to release the inner seeds, removing any bitter yellow membrane. Add the seeds and the juice to the dressing and season to taste.

Place all the salad ingredients in a bowl, pour over the dressing and toss the contents lightly together. Place on four serving plates, drizzle over any excess dressing and serve.

Roquefort-stuffed fig salad
with port vinaigrette and frozen avocado cream

Blue cheese and figs have a natural affinity – the balance of salty cheese and sweet fruit works wonderfully together. This salad is one of my favourite ways to use figs and makes an interesting dish or talking point when prepared for a dinner party, the combination of hot and cold particularly successful.

for the avocado cream

150g sugar

2 avocados (preferably Haas variety)

250ml dry white wine

juice of 1/2 lemon

4 tablespoons whipping cream

for the salad

8 large figs

120g roquefort cheese

1 tablespoon honey

1 teaspoon truffle oil (optional)

Olive oil

100g young rocket leaves

100g watercress, any tough stems removed

1 avocado, peeled, stoned and cut into small dice

50g spiced pecan nuts (see PG TIPS)

for the port vinaigrette

2 tablespoons olive oil

1 shallot, finely chopped

100ml port

3 tablespoons balsamic vinegar

1 tablespoon honey

juice of 1/2 lemon

salt and freshly ground black pepper

For the avocado cream (best made a day in advance), place the sugar and 65ml water in a pan, bring to the boil and simmer for 1 minute to make a light syrup. Leave to cool. Peel and remove the stone from the avocados, cut the flesh into pieces. Place them in a food processor with the syrup, white wine and lemon juice and blend until smooth. Add the cream, then transfer to an ice-cream machine and churn according to the manufacturer's instructions. Freeze overnight until required.

Remove a third off the top of each fig and, using a melon baller or teaspoon, scoop out a little of the flesh from the centre of each fig, taking care not to destroy their shape. Mix together the cheese, the scooped out flesh, honey and truffle oil, then stuff each fig with the mixture and replace the top back on the figs. Set aside.

For the port vinaigrette, heat the olive oil in a pan, add the shallot and cook for 30 seconds. Add the port, vinegar, honey and lemon juice and boil for 1 minute. Season to taste, pass through a sieve to remove lumps and keep warm.

Preheat the oven to 220°C/425°F/gas mark 7. Place the figs on a baking dish, drizzle over a little olive oil and place in the oven to bake for 5–6 minutes or until just softened.

Toss the rocket and watercress leaves with the diced avocado, spiced nuts and warm port dressing. Transfer the salad to serving plates. Place two stuffed figs alongside and a scoop of the avocado cream. Drizzle over a little more warm dressing and serve immediately.

PG TIPS   Spiced pecans are great for salads and easy to prepare. Simply heat some golden syrup or honey in a thick non-stick pan, add the pecan nuts and a pinch of cayenne pepper. Lightly caramelise together until golden and sticky in texture, then remove and cool them. When they are cold they will be hard and crunchy in texture. These nuts can be made in advance and are best kept in an airtight container or a biscuit tin which will stop them from going soft.

Mojo criolla-grilled vegetable salad

I love the punchy flavours in this Latin American-style salad – the tangy piquant dressing beautifully matched with grilled sweet vegetables and buttery avocado.

for the mojo criolla dressing

2 garlic cloves, crushed

1 hot red chilli, deseeded and finely chopped

1 teaspoon cumin seeds, toasted

100ml extra-virgin olive oil

50ml fresh orange juice

2 teaspoons sherry vinegar

1 teaspoon tomato ketchup

salt and freshly ground black pepper

100ml olive oil

2 large red peppers, deseeded and cut into thick strips

2 large yellow peppers, deseeded and cut into thick strips

12 baby sweetcorn

6 small courgettes, halved lengthways

12 asparagus tips

9 baby leeks, trimmed

4 palm hearts (tinned), cut into long batons

1 tablespoon superfine capers

1 avocado, peeled, stoned and cut into 1cm dice

For the dressing, place the garlic, chilli, cumin seeds and a little salt in a mortar and crush with a pestle to a smooth paste. Heat the olive oil in a pan and, when hot, add the garlic paste. Remove from the heat and leave to stand for 5 minutes, before adding the orange juice, vinegar and tomato ketchup. Season to taste, leave to cool and refrigerate until needed.

Heat a ridged grill pan until smoking. Drizzle in the olive oil and grill the peppers and baby sweetcorn for 5 minutes on each side or until the skins are blistered and charred. Transfer the peppers to a bowl, lightly cover with clingfilm and leave to steam for 20 minutes. Peel the peppers and place in a large bowl.

Place the remaining vegetables on the grill pan and grill until cooked and lightly charred. Place all the vegetables in a bowl, then add a little dressing to the vegetables and toss gently together. Add the capers and diced avocado and toss again. Place in a huge pile, drizzle over the remaining dressing and serve at room temperature.

Lasagne salad

with artichokes, avocado, fennel and mozzarella

The ultimate up-market pasta salad, thin stacked layers of pasta encasing a delicious salad of artichoke, buttery avocado and fennel. Pre-prepared or manufactured pasta sheets could be substituted if necessary.

1 teaspoon coriander seeds

pinch of fresh saffron

1 head of fennel, peeled and cut into 1cm strips

200g prepared pasta dough (see PG TIPS page 112)

olive oil

1 avocado, peeled, stoned and cut into 1cm dice

3 plum tomatoes, deseeded and cut into small dice

1 red onion, peeled and thinly sliced

100g marinated baby artichokes in oil, drained and oil reserved

100g buffalo mozzarella, cut into 1cm dice

75g watercress, tough stems removed

25g shiso cress

50g corn salad (mâche or lambs lettuce)

salt, freshly ground black pepper and nutmeg

for the dressing

1 small free-range egg yolk

1/4 teaspoon Dijon mustard

1 garlic clove, crushed

1 tablespoon balsamic vinegar

5 tablespoons reserved artichoke oil (see above)

lemon juice

salt and freshly ground black pepper

Bring 150ml water to the boil in a small pan with the coriander seeds and saffron. Add the fennel and cook for 2–3 minutes, remove it and leave to cool. Reduce the cooking liquid by half. Set aside.

For the dressing, whisk the egg yolk, mustard, garlic and vinegar in a bowl, then slowly add the reserved artichoke oil and lemon juice and season to taste. Finally add the reserved fennel stock.

For the pasta, roll out the dough several times until the machine is at its thinnest setting. Cut into twelve neat rectangles, approximately 12cm x 10cm. You may need to pass the dough through again to obtain all you need. Cook the pasta sheets in a large pan of boiling salted water for 1–2 minutes then remove them carefully with a slotted spoon into a bowl of iced water. Drain well, dry them in a clean towel and lay them out on a clean work surface. Season them with a little salt, pepper and nutmeg and brush them with a little olive oil.

Place the avocados, tomatoes, onion, artichokes, cooked fennel and diced mozzarella in a bowl and pour over a little of the prepared dressing. Toss gently together and season to taste.

To serve, lay one sheet of pasta on each serving place, top with some salad, sprinkle over the watercress, shiso and corn salad, then more pasta, more of the artichoke salad and finally a layer of pasta. Drizzle over a little more dressing. Prepare all four salads in this manner. Serve at room temperature.

Summer ruby salad

This stunning ruby-coloured salad is one of my favourite summertime preparations – a combination of sweet and peppery flavours. I always prefer to cook my own beetroot at any time, although it's fine to use the cooked varieties sold packed in stores and supermarkets. However, be sure not to buy the pickled variety.

for the dressing

4 tablespoons raspberry or red wine vinegar

1/2 teaspoon Dijon mustard

1 teaspoon maple syrup

6 tablespoons mild olive oil

salt and freshly ground black pepper

2 large cooked beetroots (see page 46), peeled and cut into 1cm dice

1 red onion, thinly sliced

8 red radishes

300g watermelon, cut into 1cm dice

100g red cabbage, very thinly sliced

20 fresh purple basil leaves

40g edible purple flowers (borage, lavender, pansies etc.)

salt and freshly ground black pepper

For the dressing, whisk together all the ingredients in a bowl and season to taste.

Place all the salad ingredients in another bowl, pour over the dressing, season to taste and toss together. Place attractively on four serving plates and serve immediately.

PG TIPS   Diced buffalo mozzarella or goat's cheese makes a good addition to this salad. I also serve the salad dressed in a horseradish crème fraîche dressing, made by whisking together 1 tablespoon of sherry vinegar with 1 tablespoon of creamed horseradish, 100ml olive oil, 3 tablespoons of crème fraîche and seasoning.

Salad of chickpeas, cauliflower and apricots
with roasted bulghur bhel phooris

Bhel phooris are a savoury snack served as a street food in Mumbai (Bombay) in India. Deliciously tasty and moreish. The idea came to me to create a salad of sorts with this in mind. The street vendors known as bhelwale have mastered the art of preparing different bhel (snacks) for generations. This is somewhat of a heretical variation with chickpeas, cauliflower and apricots, but the results are wonderful – a sweet yogurt dressing completes the dish. Puffed rice, Bombay spice mix and chat masala are available from Indian stores.

2 tablespoons olive oil

1 small onion, chopped

$1/8$ teaspoon turmeric powder

1 garlic clove, crushed

1 small cauliflower, cut into small florets

125g bulghur (cracked wheat)

$1/2$ teaspoon cumin seeds

300g cooked chickpeas (tinned are fine), drained

50g ready-to-eat dried apricots, chopped

50g roasted cashew nuts

2 tablespoons pumpkin seeds

25g puffed rice

1 packet Bombay spice mix

$1/2$ teaspoon chat masala

25g fresh coriander leaves

for the dressing

3 tablespoons tamarind paste

1 tablespoon brown sugar

1 small green chilli, finely chopped

$1/2$ teaspoon cumin powder

2 tablespoons chopped fresh mint

100ml natural yogurt

juice of $1/2$ lemon

Heat the oil in a large frying pan and, when warm, add the onion and cook until lightly softened. Add the turmeric powder, garlic and cauliflower and mix well. Add a little water, cover with a lid and cook over a gentle heat for 10–12 minutes, until the cauliflower is just cooked, retaining its shape. Remove to a bowl and leave to cool.

Clean out the frying pan and heat it again, until hot this time, then add the bulghur wheat and cumin seeds and toss them constantly until they are golden and toasted. Transfer to a bowl, pour over 600ml water, cover with clingfilm and leave to soak for 15–20 minutes, then remove the clingfilm and leave to cool.

For the dressing, combine the tamarind paste and brown sugar with 120ml water in a small pan and heat until the sugar has melted. Add the chopped chilli and the cumin powder, simmer for 5 minutes and then remove to a bowl to cool. When cool, add the mint, yogurt and lemon juice.

Add the soaked bulghur to the cauliflower, then add the chickpeas, chopped apricots, cashew nuts, pumpkin seeds and finally the puffed rice and Bombay mix. Season with a little chat masala, then pour over the sweet yogurt dressing and toss together. Place on four serving plates and scatter over the coriander leaves. Serve immediately.

Egg salad
with peanut curry dressing

During my short time promoting and cooking in the Far East, I must have tasted probably a dozen variations of Gado Gado, a Thai inspired salad of crispy vegetables in a peanut curry dressing, apparently now popular all over southern Asia. This is a sister version, made with hard-boiled eggs and a spicier accent on the sauce.

for the peanut curry dressing

150ml coconut milk

1/2 garlic clove, crushed

50g crunchy peanut butter

1 tablespoon sweet chilli sauce

juice of 1/2 lime

good pinch of curry powder

1 teaspoon vegetarian fish sauce (nuoc mam chay) – optional

4 free-range eggs

200g small new potatoes

1 carrot, peeled and sliced

75g French beans

50g beansprouts

1/2 cucumber, cut into 5mm matchstick lengths

1 small iceburg lettuce, trimmed and shredded

50g watercress, stems trimmed

75g fresh coriander leaves

2 tablespoons crispy fried shallots (see PG TIPS)

For the dressing, bring the coconut milk to the boil in a small pan, stir in the remaining ingredients and simmer for 5 minutes until the peanut butter has melted and the mixture has thickened. Leave to cool to room temperature.

Cook the eggs in a pan of boiling water for 8–10 minutes until hard-boiled, then refresh them under cold water before shelling. Cut them in half and set aside.

In separate pans, cook the potatoes, carrot and beans, keeping the carrot and beans quite crunchy in texture. The potatoes should be cooked through, drained then thickly sliced. Refresh all the vegetables in cold water and dry them.

Toss the vegetables, beansprouts, cucumber and salad leaves together in a bowl and place on four serving plates. Top with two halves of egg per person, pour over the spiced peanut curry dressing and serve, sprinkled with crispy fried shallots.

PG TIPS In Thailand and the Philippines, many dishes are topped with crispy fried shallots, which add not only flavour but texture to the dish. To prepare them, simply heat some vegetable oil to 155°C/320°F, thinly slice the shallots and dip them in the hot oil until golden. Remove with a slotted spoon onto kitchen paper, leave to drain and crisp up and use as required.

Smoked paprika feta salad
with peppers, date cigarillos and sweet lemon dressing

A Middle Eastern-inspired salad with a combination of salty and sweet flavours. The date cigarillos can be prepared in advance and frozen until needed. Some fresh figs are also great added to this salad. Sumac is a tangy seasoning that has been used for thousands of years by Middle Eastern cooks, often as a replacement for lemon or vinegar.

for the cigarillos
2 sheets filo pastry
200g ready-to-eat dates, chopped finely
vegetable oil for deep-frying

for the salad
2 tablespoons olive oil
4 red peppers, halved and deseeded
240g feta cheese, cut into large dice
1 teaspoon smoked paprika
12 black olives
1 red onion, thinly sliced
2 tablespoons flaked almonds, toasted

for the dressing
2 lemons, halved
3 tablespoons argan oil (or olive oil)
pinch of good cinnamon
1/2 garlic clove, crushed
pinch of sumac (optional)
30g chopped fresh mint
1 teaspoon caster sugar
salt and freshly ground black pepper

For the date cigarillos, lay a sheet of filo pastry onto a work surface or board and cut into four equal rectangles, keeping the remainder of the pastry covered with a damp tea towel to prevent it drying out. Lay a good spoonful of the dates at the short end of one of the filo rectangles. Tightly roll up the pastry tucking the sides in as you near the end to securely encase the filling. Seal the last 5cm of the cigarillo with a little cold water. Repeat until the filling and pastry are used up. Set aside.

Heat a ridged grill pan until very hot, brush the grill with the olive oil. Cut each pepper half into three strips lengthways. Place on the grill and cook until tender and slightly charred, turning them regularly. Remove and peel off their skin. Leave to cool, then transfer to a bowl.

For the dressing, place the lemon halves under the grill and cook for 2–3 minutes until the lemon is slightly cooked and lightly charred. Remove and cool slightly, then squeeze the juice from the lemons into a bowl and add the remaining ingredients; season to taste.

Dust the feta pieces lightly with smoked paprika. Add the olives, onion and almonds to the pepper, pour over a little of the lemon dressing and season to taste. Place the salad on a serving plate, top with the paprika-dusted feta and drizzle over the remaining dressing.

Heat the vegetable oil to 180°C/350°F, drop the date cigarillos into the hot oil and cook for 1 minute until golden and crispy. Remove from the oil and drain on kitchen paper. Garnish the salad with two cigarillos per person and serve.

Pasta and grains

Simply by taking a trip around any good food store or shop these days, you will see the vast range of pasta and grains now available for vegetarians to expand their menu options. Whether for a simple mid-week meal or an impressive dinner party course, pasta and grain dishes are generally simple and quick to make and look wonderful. Most of these recipes can be used interchangeably, using the different combinations of ingredients so you can enjoy even more recipes than you bargained for!

Three grain risotto
with pan-roasted salsify, shiitake mushrooms and vanilla-hazelnut foam

The idea of using different grains in the risotto stems from a similar dish served at the superb Union Square Café in New York. The combination of the grains adds a wonderful nutty flavour and of course it is very healthy. I sometimes add fontina to the risotto instead of parmesan and mascarpone cheese.

75g wild rice, soaked overnight

50g spelt

50g unsalted butter

1 tablespoon olive oil

250g salsify, peeled

120g shiitake mushrooms, thickly sliced

2 shallots, finely chopped

50g vialano nano risotto rice (or similar variety)

4 tablespoons dry white wine

650ml good vegetable stock, hot

25g freshly grated castelli vegetalia (parmesan-style cheese)

1 tablespoon mascarpone cheese

2 tablespoons whipping cream

salt and freshly ground black pepper

for the vanilla-hazelnut foam

2 tablespoons whole hazelnuts

100ml skimmed milk

100ml whipping cream

4 tablespoons dry white wine

1/2 vanilla pod, split and seeds removed (see PG TIPS)

40g unsalted butter

salt and freshly ground black pepper

Cook the wild rice in boiling water for 50–60 minutes or until tender. In a separate pan, cook the spelt in boiling water for 30 minutes or until tender. Drain both grains and set aside.

Heat 20g butter and the olive oil in a pan, add the salsify and cook over a moderate heat for 4–5 minutes until golden all over. Add the shiitake mushrooms and 100ml water, cover with a lid, reduce the heat and cook for a further 10 minutes. Keep warm.

Heat a further 10g butter in a heavy-based pan, add the shallots and cook for 1 minute. Add the risotto rice, the cooked wild rice and spelt and stir well to coat with the butter. Add the white wine and boil for 1 minute. Over a moderate heat, add the hot vegetable stock a ladleful at a time, only adding more once each quantity has been absorbed. The rice should be just tender, but still retain a little bite when cooked – about 25 minutes in all. Remove from the heat, add the remaining butter, the cheeses and cream and season to taste. The finished risotto should be fairly loose without being too sloppy.

For the foam, place the hazelnuts and milk in a food processor and blend until smooth. Transfer to a small pan, add the cream, wine and vanilla seeds and bring to the boil. Reduce the heat and simmer for 2 minutes, then strain through a fine strainer. Add the butter a little at a time and blitz with a hand-held blender until foaming in texture; season to taste. Place the risotto on four serving plates or bowls, top with the salsify and mushrooms and spoon over the hazelnut foam. Serve immediately.

PG TIPS To remove the inner seeds from a fresh vanilla pod, cut the pod in half lengthways, then using the back of a small knife, carefully scrape out the black inner seeds. Use the pods to make vanilla sugar by placing them in a sealed jar with caster sugar – wonderful in dessert recipes.

Roasted butternut squash and goat's cheese risotto
with almond crumble

I have more risotto recipes in my repertoire than I can mention, but this
one is my favourite. The smoky flavour of the roasted squash is offset
beautifully by the creaminess of the goat's cheese.

600ml good vegetable stock
1 stick of cinnamon
1 small bay leaf
3 fresh sage leaves
2 tablespoons olive oil
2 shallots, finely chopped
250g vialano nano risotto rice (or similar variety)
400g butternut squash, peeled and cut into large dice
100ml dry white wine
45ml whipping cream
75g mild goat's cheese, crumbled or grated
15g unsalted butter
salt and freshly ground black pepper

for the almond crumble
4 amaretti biscuits
10g unsalted butter
1/2 teaspoon ground cinnamon

Place the vegetable stock, cinnamon, bay leaf and sage in a large pan, simmer gently
for 10–15 minutes and then strain.

Heat the olive oil in a heavy-based pan, add the shallots and cook over a gentle
heat to lightly colour and caramelise them. Add the rice and the butternut squash and
toss together carefully. Pour over the white wine and stir until it has been absorbed.
Over a moderate heat, add the fragrant stock a ladleful at a time, only adding more
once each quantity has been absorbed. The rice should be just tender, but still retain
a little bite when cooked – about 20–25 minutes in all. Add the cream, goat's cheese
and butter and fold gently into the rice. The finished risotto should be fairly loose
without being sloppy. Adjust the seasoning to taste.

For the almond crumble, place the amaretti biscuits, butter and cinnamon in a
food processor and blend for a few seconds to form small pieces.

Transfer the risotto to four deep serving bowls, sprinkle the almond crumble over
the top and serve immediately.

Walnut risotto

with brown butter and taleggio crostini

An unusual way to finish a superb risotto. After preparing the risotto in the normal manner, crisp bread slices draped with fontina cheese are layered on top. A fragrant butter is poured over the cheese, heating it sufficiently to melt it. This dish is typical of the Val d'Aosta region of Italy. Taleggio cheese is one of Italy's most prized and loved cheeses and is available from good delicatessens.

225g unsalted butter

2 shallots, finely chopped

$^1/_2$ garlic clove, crushed

250g vialano nano risotto rice (or similar variety)

4 tablespoons dry white wine

750ml good vegetable stock, hot

75g walnuts, coarsely chopped

50g watercress leaves

$^1/_2$ small crusty baguette, cut into 5mm thick slices

100g taleggio cheese, thinly sliced

40g unsalted butter

salt and freshly ground black pepper

Heat the butter in a heavy-based pan over a moderate heat, add the shallots and garlic and cook for 1 minute until softened but not coloured. Add the rice and stir until well coated with the butter. Pour over the white wine and stir until it has been absorbed. Over a moderate heat, add the hot vegetable stock a ladleful at a time, only adding more once each quantity has been absorbed. The rice should be just tender, but still retain a little bite when cooked – about 20–25 minutes in all. Add the walnuts and watercress and season to taste.

Toast the bread until golden on both sides. Transfer the rice to four deep serving bowls. Top each risotto with bread slices then drape the taleggio over the bread.

In a small frying pan, heat the butter until it foams, becomes nutty in fragrance and turns hazelnut in colour. Quickly spoon over the cheese and leave for 30 seconds to allow the cheese to soften before serving.

Wild rice and parsnip suppli
with crushed cauliflower and cherry jus

Suppli is the Italian word for rice fritters. I also recommend serving this
dish with some roasted wild or portobello mushrooms. The fresh sage
can be replaced with rosemary or chopped flat-leaf parsley.

75g wild rice, soaked overnight and drained

25g unsalted butter

1 onion, finely chopped

6 sage leaves, roughly chopped

2 parsnips, peeled and grated

150g vialano nano risotto rice (or similar variety)

900ml good vegetable stock, hot

25g freshly grated castelli vegetalia
*   (parmesan-style cheese)*

50g fresh white breadcrumbs

4 tablespoons plain flour

2 free-range eggs, lightly beaten

1 cauliflower, cut into small florets

5 tablespoons olive oil

salt and freshly ground black pepper

for the cherry jus

2 tablespoons demerara sugar

4 tablespoons sherry vinegar (or red wine vinegar)

100ml port wine

150ml vegetarian jus (see page 189)

75g dried cherries

15g unsalted butter, chilled and cut into small pieces

Cook the wild rice in plenty of boiling salted water for 40–45 minutes or until tender.
Drain well and dry.

Melt the butter in a heavy-based pan, add the onion and half the sage and cook
over a low heat for about 3–4 minutes until soft. Add the parsnips and risotto rice
and cook together for 1–2 minutes. Over a moderate heat, add the hot vegetable
stock a ladleful at a time, only adding more once each quantity has been absorbed.
The rice should be just tender, but still retain a little bite when cooked – about
20–25 minutes in all. Remove from the heat, add the cheese, cooked rice,
breadcrumbs and remaining sage and mix well before turning out onto a baking tray.
Leave to cool.

Divide the mixture into eight and shape into cakes. Dip them in flour, then into
the beaten egg and refrigerate until required. (The cakes can be made to this stage a
day in advance.)

For the cherry jus, place the sugar and vinegar in a pan and lightly caramelise
together until golden. Add the port wine, vegetarian jus and dried cherries and simmer
for 10 minutes over a low heat. Add the chilled butter and swirl it into the sauce.
Keep hot.

Cook the cauliflower florets in boiling water until tender, drain them well, add
2 tablespoons of the olive oil and a little seasoning and crush them lightly with a fork.
Keep hot.

Cook the cakes in a large frying pan in the remaining olive oil for 2–3 minutes on
each side until golden. Drain on kitchen paper. Place two cooked cakes on each
serving plate on a bed of crushed cauliflower and pour around some of the cherry jus.
Serve immediately.

Goan chickpea risotto
with cashew nuts and coconut yogurt

Here is a tongue in cheek look at an Asian-style risotto that materialised
one night at home, during a hunger spell. It was rather good and so I
decided to share it with you.

for the mild curry paste

4 teaspoons garam masala

2 tablespoons mild curry powder

100g ghee or clarified butter (see PG TIPS page 171)

2 shallots, finely chopped

2 garlic cloves, crushed

125g baby spinach leaves

250g vialano nano risotto rice (or similar variety)

600ml good vegetable stock, hot

300g cooked chickpeas (tinned are fine), drained

3 tablespoons cashew nuts, toasted and roughly chopped

50g raisins, soaked in water for 30 minutes and drained

20g fresh coriander leaves

120ml coconut yogurt to serve (see page 135)

For the curry paste, place the garam masala and curry powder in a bowl and stir in
2 tablespoons of water. Set aside.

Melt the ghee or butter in a heavy-based pan, add the shallots and garlic and
cook for 2–3 minutes until softened. Add the spinach and cook for 1 minute. Add
the rice, then stir well to coat with the vegetables and butter. Stir in the curry paste
and mix well. Over a moderate heat, add the hot vegetable stock a ladleful at a time,
only adding more once each quantity has been absorbed. The rice should be just
tender, but still retain a little bite when cooked – about 20–25 minutes. Add the
chickpeas, cashews, raisins and half the coriander and cook for a further 1 minute.
Divide the rice between four serving plates, drizzle over a little of the coconut yogurt
and scatter over the remaining coriander. Serve immediately.

Pumpkin and aduki bean biryani

There are many types of biryani, flavoured with spices and cooked with meat or vegetables. It is one of the great classics of the Indian kitchen. This recipe is a variation from my friend Janmejoy Sen, restaurant chef of the Imperial New Delhi. He says the secret of a good biryani is not only in the spices, but cooking the rice in two stages to keep it light and fluffy. A mint chutney completes a great dish and can be made in advance and kept in the fridge.

200g aduki (or adzuki) beans

vegetable oil for shallow frying

2 onions, very thinly sliced

4 garlic cloves, crushed

5cm piece of ginger, peeled and chopped

350g basmati rice, rinsed and drained

75g ghee or clarified butter (see PG TIPS page 171)

2 tablespoons biryani curry paste

2 teaspoons ground cardamom

1/2 teaspoon chilli powder

1/2 teaspoon ground turmeric

350g pumpkin, peeled and cut into large pieces

1 teaspoon garam masala

juice of 1 lemon

50g flaked almonds, toasted

mint chutney (see PG TIPS) – optional

Rinse the aduki beans under cold water, place in a pan, cover with water and cook over a moderate heat for 40–45 minutes or until tender. Drain and set aside.

Heat the vegetable oil in a large pan or frying pan and, when it reaches 170°C/325°F, add the thinly sliced onions and fry until golden and slightly crisp. Remove with a slotted spoon and drain on kitchen paper.

Blitz the garlic and ginger to a paste in a blender. Place the rice into a pan of 600ml boiling water, cook for 10–12 minutes and then drain.

Melt the ghee or clarified butter in a large heavy-based pan, add half the fried onion, the garlic and ginger paste and cook over a moderate heat for 2 minutes. Add the biryani paste, cardamom, chilli powder and turmeric and cook for a further 2 minutes. Add the pumpkin and aduki beans, along with 300ml water, cover and cook for about 10 minutes until the pumpkin is just tender. Add the half-cooked rice, cover with a lid and reduce the heat to its lowest setting. Allow the steam to cook the rice for a further 8–10 minutes until tender and fluffy. Remove the lid, add the garam masala and lemon juice and toss well together. Transfer to a serving dish and top with the remaining crispy fried onions and the toasted flaked almonds and serve with the mint chutney, if desired.

PG TIPS   For a simple Indian-style mint chutney, blend together until smooth a handful of mint leaves, 1 teaspoon of sugar, 125ml natural yogurt, 1 teaspoon of tamarind paste and 1 deseeded green chilli. Season with a little cumin and refrigerate until needed. This chutney will keep for 2 days in the fridge, when it will begin to lose its colour. This chutney is good served with all manner of Indian-style dishes.

Honey-roasted vegetables
with cumin and fig couscous and olive sauce

Every honey is different, the flavour and strength determined by the flowers that the bees visit. Cheap brands all tend to taste the same, so it is worth paying that little bit extra for a good one.

for the olive sauce

120ml milk

1 garlic clove, crushed

50g ground almonds

60g fresh white breadcrumbs

50g stoned black olives, chopped

6 tablespoons olive oil

4 tablespoons yogurt

salt and freshly ground black pepper

for the honey-roasted vegetables

4 tablespoons good-quality honey

juice and zest of 1 lemon

1 aubergine, cut into 1cm dice

1 red onion, cut into wedges

2 courgettes, cut into 1cm dice

2 red peppers, cut into 1cm dice

1 yellow pepper, cut into 1cm dice

olive oil

600ml good vegetable stock, hot

salt and freshly ground pepper

for the cumin and fig couscous

350g couscous

1 teaspoon ground cumin

500ml good vegetable stock, hot

4 ripe but firm figs, cut into wedges

2 tablespoons chopped fresh mint

2 tablespoons chopped fresh flat-leaf parsley

Preheat the oven to 230°C/450°F/gas mark 8. For the olive sauce, place the milk, garlic, almonds and breadcrumbs in a food processor and blend to a smooth purée. Add the olives and blend for a further 20–30 seconds. With the motor running, gently pour in the the olive oil through the funnel at the top and continue blending until smooth. Remove to a bowl, season to taste (taking care not to add too much salt as the olives are already salty in flavour) and stir in the yogurt. Refrigerate until needed.

For the vegetables, place the honey, lemon juice and zest in a roasting tin and add the vegetables. Drizzle over some olive oil, toss well together and season lightly. Put in the oven and roast for 15 minutes until lightly caramelised, tossing them from time to time to ensure even cooking. Pour over the vegetable stock and cook for a further 20–25 minutes until the vegetables are cooked and the liquid in the tray is thick and caramelised.

Meanwhile for the couscous, place the couscous in a shallow dish. Add the cumin, pour over the hot vegetable stock to cover and stir well. Cover and leave to stand for 5–6 minutes before separating the grains with a fork. Add the fig wedges and chopped herbs. Serve with the roasted vegetables on top, drizzle over the pan juices and olive sauce. Serve immediately.

Buckwheat spaetzle

with cavalo nero, roasted chanterelles and chestnuts

Spaetzle – tender little morsels that are like a cross between a noodle and a dumpling – are common to Austrian, German and Swiss cuisine. They are excellent for absorbing creamy sauces as in this recipe. Cavolo nero (black cabbage) is a wonderful Italian cabbage – substitute with Savoy cabbage if unavailable.

for the spaetzle

275g plain flour

100g buckwheat flour

6 free-range eggs, beaten

iced water

salt and freshly ground black pepper

25g unsalted butter

1 tablespoon mild olive oil

1 shallot, finely chopped

1 garlic clove, crushed

200g chanterelle mushrooms, cleaned

1 tablespoon chopped fresh flat-leaf parsley

75g vacuum-packed chestnuts

150g cavalo nero, finely shredded

100ml double cream

1 tablespoon grated vegetarian gruyère or emmental

1 tablespoon truffle oil

For the spaetzle, sift the flour and a little salt into a large bowl and add the buckwheat flour. Make a well in the centre, tip in the beaten eggs and, using your hands or a wooden spoon, mix them into the flour with enough water to form a thick but runny batter.

Bring a large pan of salted water to the boil and top the pan with a large-holed colander (ensuring the colander does not touch the water). Pour in a little of the batter and, using a scraper or flat spatula, push the batter through the colander into the water. When the noodles rise to the surface – after about 1 minute – remove them with a slotted spoon into iced water. Prepare all the spaetzle in the same manner. Drain well in a colander and dry in a cloth.

For the vegetables, heat the butter and oil in a large frying pan over a gentle heat, add the shallot and garlic and cook until tender. Raise the heat, add the chanterelles, parsley and chestnuts and fry until golden. Add the cavalo nero, toss together, add 100ml water and cook for 3–4 minutes.

Throw in the spaetzle, toss with the vegetables and heat through. Add the cream and cheese and season to taste. Place in a serving dish, drizzle over the truffle oil and serve.

Mee krob

One of my favourite memories during my short time working in Singapore is eating this simple Asian vegetable dish of crunchy cooked vegetables, on top of a bed of crispy rice noodles.

groundnut or vegetable oil for deep-frying

125g rice vermicelli noodles

2 tablespoons vegetable oil

6 shallots, finely sliced

3 garlic cloves, crushed

1 red chilli, very thinly sliced

100g firm tofu, cut into 1cm dice (optional)

50g peanuts, chopped

1 small butternut squash, peeled and thinly sliced

100g oyster mushrooms, cut into strips

4 large spring onions, sliced thinly

100g baby sweetcorn

75g French beans, topped, tailed and blanched

75g beansprouts

2 tablespoons palm sugar (or brown sugar)

2 tablespoons rice wine vinegar (or white wine vinegar)

1 teaspoon vegetarian fish sauce (nuoc mam chay) – optional

juice of 1 lime

50g fresh coriander leaves

Heat the oil in a frying pan or large pan. When the oil is hot add the noodles, a few at a time, until puffed up and cooked – only a matter of seconds. Remove with a slotted spoon onto kitchen paper and drain thoroughly.

Heat a wok or large frying pan with 2 tablespoons of vegetable oil, add the shallots and garlic and cook until they turn golden. Add the chilli, tofu (if using), peanuts and vegetables and stir-fry for 2–3 minutes. Add the palm sugar, vinegar, fish sauce and lime juice and cook for a further 30 seconds. Divide the fried noodles between four serving plates, top with the vegetables, garnish with the coriander leaves and serve.

Black mushroom fideau

A fideau is a Spanish noodle dish, made using fideos noodles. In this
recipe, a collection of assorted wild and cultivated mushrooms cooked in
an enriched mushroom stock form the base of the dish.

for the stock

450g flat mushrooms

2 teaspoons tomato purée

2 tablespoons mild olive oil

1 onion, chopped

1 garlic clove, crushed

few coriander stalks

1.5 litres vegetable stock

2 tablespoons olive oil

1 onion, finely chopped

1 garlic clove, crushed

700g wild and cultivated mushrooms (i.e. chestnut,
*   trompettes, girolles, shiitake), cleaned and cut into pieces*

1/2 teaspoon smoked paprika

180g fideos noodles (or spaghetti)

120g orzo pasta

4 tomatoes, blanched, skinned and chopped

150ml aïoli (garlic mayonnaise) – see PG TIPS

For the base stock, place the flat mushrooms and tomato purée in a food processor
and blend to a coarse mush. Heat the olive oil in a pan, add the onion and garlic and
cook for 2–3 minutes. Add the mushroom mixture and coriander stalks and cook
over a high heat for 5 minutes, stirring regularly. Add the vegetable stock and simmer
for a further 15 minutes. Strain the stock through a fine strainer and keep hot.

Preheat the oven to 180°C/350°F/gas mark 4. Heat the olive oil in a casserole
dish, add the onions and garlic and cook for 1 minute. Throw in the mushrooms and
smoked paprika and cook over a high heat for 2 minutes. Pour over the hot
mushroom stock and bring to the boil. Stir in both pastas and the tomatoes, reduce
the heat to a simmer and cook for 6 minutes. Place in the oven for 5–6 minutes to
finish cooking and lightly crisp the surface. Leave to cool slightly. Serve with the aïoli.

PG TIPS   For the aïoli, crush 2 garlic cloves in a mortar. Add 1 egg yolk and mix.
Trickle in 150ml olive oil, stirring constantly in the same direction to mix thoroughly.
Add a little salt and a dash of lemon juice. The sauce should be thick and glossy.

My fusion noodles

A simple and quick dish to prepare when you are hungry and short of time. The flavours from the Far East and Italy blend well together; remember, it was Marco Polo who allegedly introduced pasta to the Western world, bringing it back from China.

400g Chinese egg noodles

2 tablespoons olive oil

1/2 garlic clove, crushed

1 red chilli, deseeded and finely chopped

2.5cm piece of root ginger, peeled and chopped

175g shiitake mushrooms, thinly sliced

3 tablespoons pesto sauce (see PG TIPS)

serves 6–8

Bring a large pan of water to the boil, add the noodles and cook according to the packet instructions. Drain in a colander and set aside.

Heat the oil in a large frying pan, add the garlic, chilli and ginger and cook for 1 minute. Throw in the shiitake mushrooms and cook for a further 2–3 minutes. Add the cooked noodles and toss with the mushrooms, using a pair of kitchen tongs. Finally, add the pesto sauce and toss again. Place in four serving bowls and serve immediately.

PG TIPS   For home-made pesto, place 75g fresh basil leaves, 2 peeled garlic cloves, 1 tablespoon of pine kernels, 2 tablespoons of finely grated castelli vegetalia (parmesan-style cheese) and a pinch of sugar in a blender. Blitz until finely chopped then drizzle in 100ml good-quality olive oil through the funnel and blend until almost smooth. Season to taste.

Sardinian carrot gnocchi
with minted caramelised cipollini onions and leeks

The grain fregola is Sardinia's version of couscous, and is sometimes flavoured with saffron. Commercial fregola is getting easier to find at Italian grocers and speciality food shops; it also comes in different sizes but use the smaller variety for this dish.

400g carrots, peeled and left whole

500ml milk

ground nutmeg

250g fregola (Sardinian semolina or semolina flour)

50g freshly grated castelli vegetalia (parmesan-style cheese) – plus more for garnishing

3 free-range egg yolks

25g unsalted butter, melted

salt and freshly ground black pepper

for the caramelised onions and leeks

50g unsalted butter

1 tablespoon caster sugar

300g cipollini onions, peeled

12 baby leeks, cut into 8cm lengths

1 tablespoon chopped fresh mint

Place the carrots in a pan, cover with water, bring to the boil and simmer for about 25 minutes until just tender. Drain and slice them into 2cm thick slices. Transfer to a food processor and blend until smooth. Set aside.

Heat the milk together with salt and a little nutmeg. When it boils, stir in the fregola, little by little, stirring constantly with a whisk so that lumps do not form. Once it is all incorporated, add the carrot purée and mix well. Cook on the lowest heat for 15 minutes, stirring from time to time. Remove from the heat, leave to cool for 15 minutes, then vigorously stir in 30g cheese and the egg yolks. Spread out the mixture, about 1cm thick, into a well buttered baking tin or tray and leave to cool. Preheat the oven to 220ºC/425ºF/gas mark 7.

Using a cookie cutter 5cm in diameter, cut out discs from the mixture, and place in another well buttered baking tin. Brush them liberally with melted butter, sprinkle over the remaining 20g cheese and place in the oven for about 15 minutes until the gnocchi begin to brown.

Meanwhile, for the caramelised onions, place the butter and sugar in a pan along with 250ml water and bring to the boil. Add the cipollini onions, leeks and mint and cook over a gentle heat until they are cooked and the vegetables lightly caramelised in the mint butter. Place the gnocchi on four serving plates, top with the caramelised vegetables and drizzle over the remaining cooking juices. Scatter over some cheese and serve immediately.

Purple potato gnocchi
with basil-scented spring vegetables

Gnocchi made with purple potatoes (also known as truffle potatoes) make a strikingly colourful dish. The Provençal-style vegetables make this dish a taste sensation.

for the gnocchi
900g purple potatoes, peeled

275g plain flour

1 free-range egg

salt, freshly cracked black pepper and ground nutmeg

for the vegetables
6 tablespoons extra-virgin olive oil

1 head of fennel, cut into 1cm strips

100g carrots, cut into 1cm lozenges

3 baby courgettes, cut into 1cm lozenges

75g shelled peas (or frozen)

50g shelled broad beans

1 garlic clove, crushed

2 firm but ripe tomatoes, blanched, seeded and chopped

10 fresh basil leaves

salt and freshly ground black pepper

Place the potatoes in a pan, cover with water, bring to the boil and simmer for about 25–30 minutes or until tender. Drain well and dry in a tea towel. Rub the potatoes through a fine sieve into a large bowl. Add the flour and egg and season with salt, pepper and nutmeg. Mix well together and knead to form a smooth dough. With floured hands, roll the dough into long 2cm diameter cylinders, then cut into 2cm pieces. Using a fork, make an indentation on each piece. Place the rolled gnocchi on a floured tray until ready to cook.

For the vegetables, heat half the olive oil in a large pan, add the fennel and cook over a low heat, covered, for 5–6 minutes. Then add the carrots, courgettes and 30ml water and cook for a further 10 minutes or until the vegetables are just tender. Add the peas and broad beans and cook for a further 5 minutes. After cooking there should be about 4 tablespoons of liquid left. Pour in the remaining oil, garlic and tomatoes and season to taste, then cook for a final 2 minutes. Stir in the basil and keep warm.

Bring a large saucepan of salted water to the boil, reduce the heat, add the gnocchi and poach for 3–4 minutes or until they rise to the surface of the water. Drain them well. Place the gnocchi in four serving bowls, pour over the vegetables and season with a little cracked black pepper and serve.

Sweet potato and coconut polenta
with Asian vegetable fricassé

An Asian-Italian twist on polenta, flavoured with coconut milk, which
provides the perfect base for the quickly cooked Asian vegetable medley.

450ml good vegetable stock

1 large sweet potato, peeled and cut into small dice

600ml coconut milk

50g unsalted butter

175g quick-cook polenta

salt and freshly ground black pepper

for the vegetables

2 tablespoons vegetable oil

15g unsalted butter

1 garlic clove, crushed

1cm piece of root ginger, peeled and finely chopped

100g shiitake mushrooms, sliced

2 courgettes, sliced diagonally

1 small head of broccoli, cut into small florets

120g sugar snap peas, sliced diagonally

100ml good vegetable stock

4 tablespoons sweet chilli sauce

serves 6–8

Place the vegetable stock and diced sweet potato in a pan, bring to the boil and simmer for 12–15 minutes until the potato is tender. Transfer to a food processor and blend until smooth. Return to the pan, add the coconut milk and half the butter and bring to a rolling boil. Pour in the polenta, stirring constantly, lower the heat and simmer for 5–8 minutes until the polenta comes away from the sides of the pan, with the consistency of wet mashed potato. Stir in the remaining butter, season to taste and keep warm.

For the vegetables, heat the oil and butter in a wok or frying pan over a moderate heat, add the garlic and ginger and cook for 30 seconds. Add the vegetables, toss together for 2 minutes, then add the vegetable stock and sweet chilli sauce. Pour the wet polenta onto four serving plates or bowls and top with the vegetables. Serve immediately.

Tomato, spinach and basil sformatino

An impressive Mediterranean polenta gâteau, which is light and delicious and full of gutsy flavours. Any leftovers make a great base, pan-fried and then topped with goat's cheese or mozzarella.

1 litre full-fat milk

4 garlic cloves, crushed

200g quick-cook polenta

150g butter

2 red chillies, deseeded and finely chopped

1 onion, finely chopped

100g fresh spinach leaves

75g fresh basil leaves (plus more for garnishing)

2 tablespoons pine nuts, toasted

150g sunblush tomatoes in oil, drained and chopped

2 free-range eggs, separated

salt, freshly ground black pepper and ground nutmeg

900g loaf tin

serves 6–8

Preheat the oven to 180ºC/350ºF/gas mark 4. Place the milk and half the garlic in a pan and bring to the boil. Stir in the polenta and cook over a low heat for 2–3 minutes, stirring constantly. Divide the polenta into two equal amounts.

Melt 75g butter in a frying pan, add the remaining garlic, the chillies, onion and spinach leaves and cook over a high heat for 2–3 minutes until tender and all the liquid from the spinach has evaporated. Add the basil, mix well, then place in a food processor and blend to a coarse purée or chop finely with a knife. Add the mixture to one half of the polenta. Add the pine nuts and chopped sunblush tomatoes to the other half of the polenta. Season both polentas to taste with salt, pepper and a little nutmeg. Mix the egg yolks and whip the whites separately, and add equal amounts of yolk and whites to each polenta.

Heavily grease a loaf tin and then put in alternating layers of both polentas until you reach the top. Tap down to exclude any air. Place in the oven to bake for 12–15 minutes until well risen and golden. Leave to cool slightly before demoulding to allow it to set. Slice into equal portions and place on serving plates.

Melt the remaining butter in a frying pan, add some basil and 2 tablespoons of water and cook for 1 minute until emulsified. Pour a little around each slice and serve.

Orecchiette

with chickpeas, broccoli rabe, garlic, basil and olive oil

Orrechiette (or ear-shaped pasta) are made from flavoured durum wheat semolina and can be difficult to perfect, especially the shaping technique. Delicatessens seem to sell good-quality ones, so it is sometimes not worth making them yourself. For all you enthusiasts and foodies, I include a recipe for fresh orecchiette anyway. If using bought orrechiette you will need 400g for this recipe. If you can't find broccoli rabe, then use any kind of greens.

for the orecchiette

200g '00' pasta flour

100g durum wheat semolina

2 tablespoons olive oil

200ml warm water

salt

for the sauce

300g broccoli rabe

400g orrechiette pasta (home-made or bought)

4 tablespoons extra-virgin olive oil

2 garlic cloves, crushed

1 red onion, halved and thinly sliced

pinch of red chilli flakes

200g cooked chickpeas (tinned are fine), drained

10 fresh basil leaves, torn in pieces

6 fresh mint leaves, torn in pieces

freshly grated castelli vegetalia (parmesan-style cheese) – optional

salt and freshly ground black pepper

For the freshly made orrechiette, mix together the flour and semolina and make a well in the centre. Add a pinch of salt, the olive oil and water. Work in the flour from the edges and knead the dough for at least 10 minutes, then place in a lightly floured bowl, cover with a tea towel and leave to stand for 30 minutes. Divide the dough into four and roll into long strips 1cm in diameter, then cut each roll into 1-cm pieces and roll these into balls. Flatten each ball with the thumb so that the dough resembles an earlobe. Place on a floured tea towel, cover and leave to dry for a few hours.

For the sauce, cut the broccoli rabe into small florets and the stalk into large pieces. Cook it in plenty of boiling salted water for 4–5 minutes – it should be fairly well cooked. Remove and drain in a colander.

Cook the orrechiette in a large pan of boiling salted water for about 4–5 minutes, remove and drain.

Heat the olive oil in a large frying pan, add the garlic, onion and chilli flakes and cook over a low heat for 4–5 minutes or until the onion is tender. Add the orrechiette, cooked broccoli and chickpeas and gently toss together. Scatter over the herbs, season to taste and serve. Serve the grated cheese separately if preferred.

Olive polenta

with vegetable gratin and salsa verde

Polenta is a staple of north Italian cookery and, whether served creamy
soft or simply grilled, it makes a great base for many wonderful dishes.
A good tip for dicing the dolcelatte is to freeze it for 1 hour before cutting.

1 litre good vegetable stock

300g quick-cook polenta

50g stoned black olives, finely chopped

2 tablespoons extra-virgin olive oil

1 head of fennel, peeled and cut into wedges

1 small butternut squash, peeled and cut into wedges

100g dolcelatte cheese, cut into small dice

1 tablespoon pine nuts, toasted

salt and freshly ground black pepper

for the salsa verde

*50g mixed fresh herbs (basil, mint, flat-leaf parsley),
    chopped*

1 tablespoon capers, rinsed and drained

1 teaspoon Dijon mustard

2 garlic cloves, crushed

1 tablespoon white wine vinegar

100ml extra-virgin olive oil

Preheat the oven to 180°C/350°F/gas mark 4. Bring the vegetable stock to the boil,
pour in the polenta and keep stirring constantly. Reduce the heat and cook for
5–6 minutes until the mixture thickens and begins to leave the sides of the pan. Stir
in the olives.

Grease a baking tray with a little olive oil, spread the polenta into a 24cm square
then flatten and level off with a palette knife. Place in the fridge to set.

Blanch the fennel wedges in boiling water for 3–4 minutes, then remove and
drain well. Place in a baking tin along with the butternut squash. Drizzle over a
little olive oil and season well. Roast in the oven for 15–20 minutes until golden
and tender.

For the salsa verde, place all the ingredients except the oil in a blender and blitz
until combined. Add the oil and blitz quickly until blended, keeping it fairly coarse.
Preheat a grill to its highest setting.

Cut the polenta into four large triangles. Brush the triangles with a little olive oil
and place under the hot grill until golden and crusty. Remove the vegetables from the
oven and arrange them on the polenta triangles. Top each triangle with some diced
dolcelatte and return to the grill for 2 minutes or until softened.

Serve the vegetable polenta wedges on four serving plates, top with a good
spoonful of salsa verde and garnish with toasted pine nuts.

Rolled wild garlic and pumpkin lasagne
with pesto cream

Wild garlic has a short growing season during the spring months. If unavailable, chives mixed with a little garlic could be used instead. You are probably confused by a rolled lasagne, but why not? All the flavours of a classic lasagne are rolled tightly in this pasta dish to great effect.

400g pumpkin (or butternut squash), peeled, deseeded and cut into large pieces

6 tablespoons olive oil

3 tablespoons chopped fresh wild garlic

200g ricotta cheese, well drained

1 tablespoon double cream

4 tablespoons fresh white breadcrumbs

1 quantity of pasta dough made into 12 fresh lasagne sheets (see PG TIPS)

2 tablespoons freshly grated castelli vegetalia (parmesan-style cheese)

salt and freshly ground black pepper

For the pesto cream

45g fresh flat-leaf parsley

2 tablespoons chopped fresh rosemary leaves

2 garlic cloves

45g blanched almonds

2 tablespoons olive oil

25g freshly grated castelli vegetalia

25g unsalted butter

25g plain flour

300ml whole or soy milk

4 tablespoons double cream

salt and freshly ground black pepper

Preheat the oven to 190°C/375°F/gas mark 5. Place the pumpkin in a roasting tin, drizzle over the olive oil and cook in the oven for 25 minutes until the flesh is tender. Remove and leave to cool. Reduce the oven to 150°C/ 300°F/gas mark 2.

For the pesto cream, place the herbs, garlic, almonds and olive oil in a blender and blitz to a coarse paste. Stir in the parmesan. Melt the butter in a pan, stir in the flour, cook for 1–2 minutes, then add the milk and bring to the boil. Stir constantly with a whisk, reduce the heat and simmer for 2–3 minutes until thickened, smooth and glossy. Add the cream and the pesto and stir well; season to taste.

In a bowl, mix the wild garlic, ricotta, cream, pumpkin and breadcrumbs and season to taste.

Cook the lasagne sheets in boiling water until al dente, then transfer to cold water. Drain and pat the pasta sheets dry with a cloth. Divide the pumpkin mixture equally between the lasagne sheets, ensuring it covers them completely. Roll up like a Swiss roll, starting from one short end. Lightly grease a suitable ovenproof dish, then arrange the filled lasagne rolls in it. Pour the pesto sauce over the rolls, ensuring they are completely covered. Scatter over the parmesan, then place in the oven to bake for 15–20 minutes until the top is golden and slightly crusty on top. Leave to cool slightly before serving.

PG TIPS   For the basic pasta recipe, place 250g '00' flour, salt, 2 large beaten eggs, 1 large beaten egg yolk, 1 tablespoon of olive oil and 1 tablespoon of water in a food processor and blend to mix for a few seconds – it is important not to overwork the dough. Remove from the processor. Knead the dough until soft and pliable, then wrap in clingfilm and put in the fridge for 1 hour to rest. Roll out the dough and then make it into whatever shape is desired.

For lasagne sheets, use the basic pasta recipe and roll out the dough. Using a sharp knife or plain pasta wheel cut the dough into 12 x 7.5cm rectangles.

Crushed potato and bitter greens cannelloni
with white bean and rosemary ragoût

In Italy salad greens are often used in pasta dishes to great effect.

for the ragoût

400g haricot beans, soaked overnight and drained

4 tablespoons olive oil

1 small onion, finely chopped

1 carrot, cut into small dice

2 garlic cloves, crushed

pinch of red chilli flakes

1 tablespoon chopped fresh rosemary

100ml dry white wine

200g sunblush tomatoes, chopped

600g new potatoes, scrubbed

2 tablespoons mild olive oil

2 garlic cloves, crushed

50g rocket leaves, stems trimmed

50g watercress leaves

175g dolcelatte cheese

12 fresh lasagne sheets (see PG TIPS page 112)

*100ml pesto sauce (bought or home-made – see
  PG TIPS page 103)*

salt, freshly ground black pepper and ground nutmeg

serves 6–8

For the ragoût, place the soaked beans in a large pan, cover with cold water, bring to the boil, reduce the heat and simmer for 1–1^1/2 hours or until the beans are tender, adding more water if necessary. Drain the beans, reserving their cooking liquid.

Heat half the olive oil in a pan, add the onion, carrot, garlic, chilli flakes and rosemary and cook for 3–4 minutes or until the carrots have softened. Add the white wine and bring to the boil, boil for 2 minutes, before returning the beans and 150ml of the bean cooking liquid to the pan along with the tomatoes. Cook for a further 5 minutes, then stir in the remaining olive oil and season to taste. (This ragoût can be made in advance and reheated when needed.)

Cook the new potatoes in boiling salted water for about 20 minutes until tender and then drain. Heat the olive oil in a pan, add the garlic, rocket and watercress and cook for 1 minute until wilted. Add the potatoes and lightly crush them together. Transfer to a bowl and leave to cool. Once cool, mix with the dolcelatte and season to taste with salt, pepper and nutmeg.

Cook the lasagne sheets in boiling water until al dente, then transfer to cold water. Drain and pat the pasta sheets dry with a cloth. Season the pasta sheets. Fill them with the potato mixture, roll them up and brush with a little olive oil. Reheat the cannelloni in a hot oven (or 30 seconds in the microwave on a plate covered with clingfilm). Reheat the bean ragoût and divide between four serving bowls, top each with three cannelloni, drizzle over a little pesto sauce and serve immediately.

Pumpkin cappelletti
with pumpkin crisps and curried carrot cream

These little hats are surprisingly easy to make, but do take a while to prepare. For this recipe I use Asian wonton wrappers, which work extremely well.

for the cappelletti

400g piece of pumpkin (or butternut squash), peeled, deseeded and cut into large chunks

1 tablespoon mild olive oil

$1/2$ teaspoon fennel seeds, lightly crushed

1 free-range egg yolk

2 amaretti biscuits, crushed

25g fresh white breadcrumbs

$1/2$ teaspoon Thai red curry paste

2 tablespoons mango chutney, finely chopped

24 wonton wrappers

salt, freshly ground black pepper and ground nutmeg

for the pumpkin crisps

150g wedge of pumpkin, peeled

vegetable oil for deep-frying

for the curried carrot cream

2 carrots, cut into small dice

150ml good vegetable stock

1 teaspoon Thai red curry paste

6 tablespoons double cream

15g unsalted butter

few fresh coriander leaves, chopped

Preheat the oven to 200°C/400°F/gas mark 6. Place the pumpkin in a roasting tin and sprinkle over the oil, fennel seeds and a little seasoning. Roast for 25 minutes, turning them over once or twice. Remove and leave to cool. Place the pumpkin in a bowl and crush with a fork. Stir in the egg yolk, biscuits, breadcrumbs, curry paste and mango chutney and mix well; season to taste with salt, pepper and nutmeg. Refrigerate until needed.

For the crisps, using a swivel vegetable peeler, pare long thin strips off the pumpkin, then deep-fry in hot (150°C/300°F) vegetable oil, four or five strips at a time until golden and crisp. Drain on kitchen paper and set aside.

For the cappelletti, lay out the wonton wrappers on a flat surface, place $1/2$ tablespoon of filling in the centre of each square. Brush the exterior of each square with a little water and fold over each square on the diagonal. Press the sides to seal. Hold one corner on the long side between thumb and index finger. Wrap around and press the two corners together. Place on a lightly floured tray and leave to dry for 30 minutes.

For the curried carrot cream, cook the diced carrot in the vegetable stock with the curry paste for 10 minutes. Transfer to a food processor and blend to a purée. Return to the pan, add the cream and butter and bring to the boil. Season to taste, add some coriander and keep warm.

Cook the cappelletti in a large pan of boiling salted water for 3–4 minutes, then remove and drain well. Season and then toss with the curried carrot cream. Place on four serving plates, top with the pumpkin crisps and serve.

Green pea ravioli

with saffron butter and truffled beetroot salad

Fresh peas are obviously a lot more work for the preparation of these ravioli, but really do make a difference. This dish always makes an appearance on my menu when the first peas come into season in spring.

for the green pea ravioli

300g fresh shelled peas (or frozen)

20g fresh mint leaves

100g good-quality ricotta cheese, well drained

2 spring onions, finely chopped

1 tablespoon freshly squeezed lemon juice

1 recipe pasta dough (see PG TIPS page 112)

salt and freshly ground black pepper

for the saffron butter sauce

150ml good vegetable stock

100ml water from the cooking peas

100ml double cream

good pinch of good-quality saffron (or $^1/_2$ teaspoon powdered)

40g unsalted butter, chilled and cut into small pieces

salt and freshly ground black pepper

for the truffled beetroot salad

1 tablespoon balsamic vinegar

pinch of sugar

$^1/_2$ tablespoon truffle oil

1 medium-sized beetroot, cooked, peeled and cut into julienne strips (see PG TIPS)

1 truffle, cut into julienne strips (optional)

50g pea shoots

serves 6–8

For the ravioli, cook the peas in just enough boiling water to cover them for 5–6 minutes until tender and then drain (reserving 100ml of the cooking water). Refresh in iced water, drain again and dry them well. Place in a food processor with the mint, ricotta and spring onions and blend to a coarse purée. Remove to a bowl, season to taste and add the lemon juice.

Roll out the pasta into thin sheets, then brush a sheet with water and place tablespoons of the pea-ricotta mixture on it, about 5cm apart in rows. Cover with a second sheet of pasta, press down gently around the fillings, then cut the pasta into squares with a fluted or plain pasta wheel or sharp knife. Check to ensure the edges are well sealed, place on a lightly floured tray and leave to dry for 20 minutes.

For the saffron butter, heat the vegetable stock, reserved pea cooking liquid, cream and saffron in a pan and simmer until the liquid has reduced by half. Remove from the heat, whisk in the chilled butter, season to taste and then strain through a fine strainer.

Cook the ravioli in plenty of simmering salted water for 3–4 minutes until al dente, then remove with a slotted spoon and drain well.

For the salad, whisk together the vinegar, sugar and oil, add the beetroot and fresh truffle and adjust the seasoning; mix well.

To serve, divide the ravioli between four serving dishes, pour over the saffron sauce, top with the beetroot salad and pea shoots and serve immediately.

PG TIPS   To cut the beetroot into julienne strips, simply cut the beetroot into 3mm thick slices on a kitchen mandolin or with a knife. Stack three or four of the slices on top of each other, then slice them again, 3mm thick.

Porcini pappardelle
with grilled figs

Dried porcini have a wonderful robust quality about their flavour. Here they make the base for a delicate wild mushroom pasta, which you will enjoy making again and again.

for the porcini pappardelle

25g dried porcini mushrooms

2 garlic cloves, crushed

3 tablespoons extra-virgin olive oil

450g '00' pasta flour

3 free-range eggs

3 tablespoons olive oil

175g fresh porcini (or 50g soaked and dried)

1 small mild red chilli, deseeded and finely chopped

6 firm but ripe purple figs, cut into wedges

$1/2$ teaspoon caster sugar

2 tablespoons balsamic vinegar

50g freshly grated castelli vegetalia (parmesan-style cheese)

juice of $1/2$ lemon

salt, freshly ground black pepper and ground nutmeg

serves 6–8

For the pasta, soak the porcini mushrooms in warm water for 20 minutes, reserving the soaking liquid. Rinse the mushrooms well and chop very finely. Mix with the garlic and oil. Sift the flour into a bowl. Make a well in the centre, add the mushroom mixture and eggs, draw in the flour and gradually mix together to form a pliable dough. Knead for 10–12 minutes until smooth and elastic. Wrap the dough in clingfilm and leave to rest for 1 hour. Divide the dough into four, then, working one piece at a time, roll it out until paper thin. Sprinkle with a little flour, then roll up. With a sharp knife, cut the roll widthways into 2cm wide ribbons. Unroll the ribbons and lay out on a lightly floured tray. Leave to dry for 30 minutes.

Preheat a grill to its highest setting. Heat a frying pan with $1\,1/2$ tablespoons of olive oil, add the fresh porcini and chilli and cook over a high heat until the mushrooms are cooked and golden. Dust the figs with a little sugar, place on a baking sheet, place under the grill and cook until lightly caramelised. (Alternatively this can be done in a small frying pan.)

Put the reserved mushroom soaking liquid and 1.5 litres water in a large pan and bring to the boil. Cook the pasta for 3 minutes, or until al dente and drain well. Add the pasta to the mushrooms, stir in the vinegar and fold in the parmesan. Toss together, add the lemon juice and season with salt, pepper and nutmeg and arrange on serving plates. Top with caramelised fig wedges and drizzle over the remaining olive oil and serve.

Spaghetti cacio e pepe

For this dish you will need to buy a 'chitarra' or spaghetti guillotine, available from good cookery shops or you can use the flat thinnest cutter of a pasta roller. If not, substitute with good-quality bought spaghetti.

1 recipe pasta dough (see PG TIPS page 112) or
   400g dried spaghetti
1 tablespoon fresh black peppercorns
1 teaspoon pink peppercorns, rinsed
175g freshly grated pecorino romano cheese
salt

Prepare the dough in the normal manner but rest for 30 minutes. Divide the dough into four and roll out each piece through the thinnest cutters of a pasta roller. Cut the rolled pasta to fit the chitarra and trim the edges neatly. Using a rolling pin, roll out the pasta through the strings to create the spaghetti. Carefully remove the spaghetti and place on a lightly floured tray and leave to dry for 30 minutes. Lightly crush the black peppercorns in a mortar or coffee/spice grinder. Cook the spaghetti in a large pan of boiling salted water for 2–3 minutes or until al dente, then drain the pasta, reserving 150ml cooking water. Heat a large frying pan over a low heat, add half the crushed peppercorns and the pink peppercorns and cook for 30 seconds, stirring constantly. Add the reserved cooking water and pecorino and heat for a further 30 seconds. Add the pasta, toss gently together, season with a little salt and divide between four serving bowls. Sprinkle over the remaining black pepper and serve.

Saffron-cooked spaghetti
with baby spinach and fennel

Cooking the spaghetti in saffron water gives this dish an unbelievable colour as well as taste.

1 recipe pasta dough (see PG TIPS page 112) or
   400g dried spaghetti
4 tablespoons extra-virgin olive oil
1 head of fennel, finely sliced, fronds removed
1 onion, thinly sliced
200g baby spinach leaves
5 tablespoons balsamic vinegar
2 good pinches of fresh saffron
75g pecorino romano cheese, grated
salt, freshly ground black pepper and ground nutmeg

Make the spaghetti as above. Heat half the oil in a large frying pan. Add the fennel slices and onion and sauté over a moderate heat for 8–9 minutes or until soft and golden. Add the spinach and cook until it wilts, then add the balsamic vinegar.

Bring 1 litre water to the boil in a large pan, add the saffron and leave to simmer for 5 minutes for the saffron to infuse the water. Cook the spaghetti in the saffron water for 2–3 minutes or until al dente. Drain well, reserving 120ml cooking water. Add the reserved water to the vegetables and cook for 2–3 minutes. Add the cooked spaghetti, half the pecorino, toss well and season with salt, freshly ground black pepper and nutmeg. Place in four individual pasta bowls, top with the remaining pecorino, garnish with the reserved fennel fronds and serve immediately.

Tagliatelle with caramelised chicory
and deep-fried lemon zest

Either make your own pasta for this dish or buy one of the many fresh varieties available in supermarkets – the quality is generally very good.

3 lemons

4 heads of white chicory (Belgian endive)

50g unsalted butter

1 teaspoon sugar

50g raisins, soaked in hot water for 30 minutes and drained

100ml double cream

500g fresh or dried tagliatelle pasta

50g freshly grated castelli vegetalia (parmesan-style cheese)

100ml vegetable oil

salt and freshly ground black pepper

serves 6–8

Zest the lemons and place the zest into a small bowl. Halve the lemons and squeeze the juice over the zest, leave for 20 minutes to marinate and accentuate the flavour.

Remove and discard any tough or blemished outer leaves from the chicory. Trim a thin slice from the root ends, halve the chicory lengthways and then shred crossways into strips. Set aside. Melt the butter in a pan, add the chicory, sugar, little salt and pepper and sauté over a moderate heat for about 15 mintues, stirring occasionally, until the chicory is golden and caramelised. Add the raisins and cream. Remove the lemon zest from the juices, dry them in a cloth and add the juice to the chicory. Simmer for about 1–2 minutes until the sauce thickens. Keep warm.

Cook the tagliatelle in a large pan of boiling salted water for 2–3 minutes or until al dente, then drain, reserving 100ml cooking water. Add the water to the lemon cream. Toss the sauce with the pasta and half the cheese and season to taste.

Heat the vegetable oil in a small pan and add the lemon zest and fry for about 1 minute until lightly golden and crisp. Drain on kitchen paper. Place the pasta into four individual serving bowls, sprinkle over the remaining cheese and scatter over the crispy fried lemon. Serve immediately.

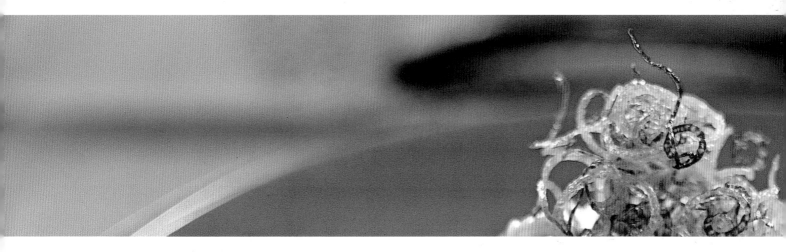

Tagliatelle with creamy brie
and sunblush tomatoes

25g unsalted butter

1 shallot, finely chopped

1/2 garlic clove, crushed

1 teapoon fresh thyme leaves

200g sunblush tomatoes in oil, drained

500g fresh or dried tagliatelle

100ml crème fraîche or double cream

150g Somerset brie, rind removed, sliced

salt and freshly ground black pepper

serves 6–8

Melt the butter in a pan, add the shallot and garlic and cook over a low heat for 5 minutes. Add the thyme and tomatoes, increase the heat and cook for about 2 minutes until softened. Cook the tagliatelle in boiling salted water until al dente and drain well. Add the crème fraîche and brie to the tomatoes and stir until melted. Return the pasta to the pan, pour over the sauce and toss together. Season to taste and serve.

PG TIPS   Use a mixture of different tagliatelle, such as plain and spinach.

Fettucine with nettles
and garlic butter

Having fallen into many stinging nettles as a child, you can imagine my horror to find you used them in cooking! Perhaps it's our way of getting them back. During the spring, nettles are at their best and most delicate. Ideally they should be no larger than the palm of your hand. Once picked, they lose their potency, and once cooked have no symptoms at all.

125g young stinging nettles, leaves only, plus 12 leaves
   for the PG TIPS (pick them using sturdy gloves)

450g fresh or dried fettucine pasta

75g unsalted butter

3 garlic cloves, crushed

1 teaspoon fennel seeds

50g grated castelli vegetalia (parmesan-style cheese)

salt and freshly ground black pepper

serves 6–8

Chop the nettle leaves coarsely. Cook the fettucine in a large pan of boiling salted water until al dente. Drain and return to the pan. While the pasta is cooking, heat the butter in a heavy-based frying pan over a low heat until the butter is foaming. Add the garlic and fennel seeds and cook for 30 seconds. Add the nettles and cook for a further 1 minute. Add the butter to the pasta, scatter over the castelli vegetalia and season. Toss well together and serve immediately.

PG TIPS   A nice idea is to top the pasta with some crispy deep-fried nettle leaves. Simply shallow-fry about twelves leaves in a pan of hot olive oil until crisp. Drain on kitchen paper.

Hot aubergine pasta
with black beans and peanut butter sauce

The Chinese black beans called for in this recipe are soya beans that have
been fermented and salted.

450g fresh or dried penne pasta

4 tablespoons vegetable or sunflower oil

1 tablespoon sesame oil

1 aubergine, cut into 1cm dice

2.5cm piece of root ginger, peeled and finely chopped

1 garlic clove

2 tablespoons dried Chinese black beans, chopped

1 small green chilli, deseeded and finely chopped

1 tablespoon sugar

2 tablespoons hoisin sauce

1 tablespoon smooth peanut butter

3 spring onions, finely chopped

2 tablespoons chopped fresh coriander

serves 6–8

Cook the penne in a large pan of boiling salted water until al dente and drain well.
Heat both oils in a wok or large frying pan, add the diced aubergine, ginger and garlic
and stir-fry over a low heat for 2–3 minutes. Add the black beans and green chilli and
stir for a further 2 minutes. Add the sugar, hoisin sauce and peanut butter and cook
until reduced and thickened. Add the pasta to the sauce and then the spring onions
and coriander. Stir until heated through and serve immediately.

Funghi carbonara

450g bucatini pasta (or spaghetti)

25g unsalted butter

20g dried wild mushrooms, soaked for 1 hour in water

1 shallot, finely chopped

150ml double cream

2 free-range eggs, beaten

100g grated castelli vegetalia (parmesan-style cheese)

salt, freshly ground black pepper and ground nutmeg

serves 6–8

Cook the spaghetti in a large pan of boiling salted water until al dente and drain well.
Heat the butter in a large frying pan, add the mushrooms and shallot and sauté for
3–4 minutes until softened. Add the cream, bring to the boil and cook for 2–3
minutes or until the sauce has thickened lightly. Add the pasta and stir in the beaten
eggs and castelli vegetalia. Toss well together and season with salt, pepper and
nutmeg. Serve immediately.

Twice-baked macaroni and celeriac soufflé

with gruyère fondue

A dish to tempt the most jaded of vegetarian palates. This one derives from the classic Roux brothers recipe enjoyed by diners at Le Gavroche for many years. The beauty of this recipe is that they can be made in advance (or even frozen if desired). In my recipe, pasta and celery root is added to the basic recipe. It's delicious served as a starter or, doubled-up, as a wonderful main dish.

275g celeriac, peeled and cut into large dice

200g macaroni pasta (or sedani pasta)

45g unsalted butter

45g plain flour

600ml milk

5 free-range egg yolks

150g roquefort cheese, crumbled

6 free-range egg whites

600ml double cream

200g finely grated gruyère cheese

salt, freshly ground black pepper and ground nutmeg

8 x 8cm diameter tartlet moulds or soufflé dishes

serves 8

Place the celeriac in a pan, cover with boiling water and simmer for about 18–20 minutes until tender. Drain well and mash until smooth.

Cook the macaroni in a large pan of boiling salted water until al dente. Refresh in cold water and drain well in a colander. Season with salt, pepper and nutmeg.

Preheat the oven to 200°C/400°F/gas mark 6. Melt the butter in a heavy-based pan, add the flour and cook over a low heat for 1 minute. Add the milk, whisking all the time to prevent lumps and, when smooth, cook for a further 3–4 minutes. Remove from the heat and allow to cool slightly before beating in the egg yolks; season to taste. Stir in the roquefort and celeriac and keep warm.

Whisk the egg whites until firm, but not stiff. Add one third of the whisked whites to the celeriac mixture, then gently fold in the remaining egg whites. Finally fold in the cooked pasta, then spoon into four well buttered tartlet moulds or soufflé dishes. Place them in the oven for 12–13 minutes only, until the top of the soufflé begins to turn golden. Remove (and cool if you are making in advance) and turn out the soufflés into individual gratin dishes.

Heat the double cream over a moderate heat and stir in the gruyère cheese. Pour the fondue over the soufflés, then return to the oven for a further 5 minutes before serving immediately.

PG TIPS For a little extra texture, you could top each soufflé with crisp cheese cracknel (see page 38).

Naked spinach ravioli
with macaroni and vegetable arrabiata dressing

In this recipe the ravioli filling is detached from its pasta casing, which is served alongside in the form of macaroni. These are the lightest of spinach dumplings imaginable, topped with a deliciously spicy dressing.

350g fresh spinach, washed and stalks removed

190g good-quality ricotta cheese, well drained

1 free-range egg

300g plain flour

40g freshly grated castelli vegetalia (parmesan-style cheese)

200g macaroni pasta (1cm thick)

salt, freshly ground black pepper and nutmeg

for the vegetable arrabiata dressing

100ml olive oil

2 shallots, finely chopped

2 garlic cloves, crushed

2 small dried red chillies, finely chopped

1 large courgette, finely diced

6 tomatoes, blanched, skinned, deseeded and chopped

2 tablespoons stoned, chopped black olives

juice of $1/2$ lemon

50g chopped fresh coriander

salt and freshly ground black pepper

Cook the spinach in a heated frying pan until wilted in its own juices. Transfer to a colander and squeeze out any excess liquid. Place in a blender and blitz to a purée. Transfer to a bowl. Add the ricotta, egg, flour and parmesan, season with salt, pepper, and nutmeg and stir. (If it's too dry add 2 tablespoons of cold water.) Cover with clingfilm and refrigerate for 1 hour.

For the dressing, heat the olive oil in a pan, add the shallots, garlic and chillies and cook over a moderate heat for 30 seconds. Raise the heat, add the courgettes and fry for 2 minutes. Add the tomatoes and olives and cook for a further 2–3 minutes. Add the lemon juice and coriander and season to taste. Keep warm.

To make the dumplings, use floured hands to roll the spinach mix into small 1cm balls. Bring a large pan of salted water to the boil, then carefully drop the dumplings into the water. When they rise to the surface (after a few minutes), remove them with a slotted spoon and drain well. Meanwhile, cook the macaroni in a large pan of boiling salted water until al dente. Toss the dumplings and pasta in the dressing, season to taste and divide between four serving bowls. Serve immediately.

Main dishes

Most people judge a style or type of cookery on the strength of the main course. The recent movement of vegetarian cookery has been to lighten dishes, use more digestible textures and include brighter and bolder seasonings inspired by cuisines from around the world. The care and preparation of main dishes make such a difference to the visual appeal of a meal and thus diner satisfaction. In this chapter, I hope you will enjoy my choice of varied dishes produced with seasonal prime vegetables.

Cauliflower and date tagine
with Tunisian pilaff

For many people dates are too sweet and should only be confined to sticky-based Middle Eastern-style pastries – not so! Within this north African cauliflower tagine they are wonderful, working in harmony with the delicate spices. Dates have been a staple food in desert lands for thousands of years.

1 large cauliflower, cut into florets

1 tablespoon plain flour

1/2 teaspoon chilli powder

1 teaspoon ground coriander

1 teaspoon ground ginger

good pinch of ground turmeric

4 tablespoons olive oil

1 onion, chopped

1 garlic clove, crushed

400g tin peeled tomatoes, chopped

100g stoned dates

750ml good vegetable stock

3 tablespoons chopped fresh coriander

2 tablespoons chopped fresh mint

salt and freshly ground black pepper

for the Tunisian pilaff

2 tablespoons olive oil

50g whole blanched almonds

1 onion, chopped

50g currants

1 teaspoon ground cinnamon

350g long-grain rice

750ml good vegetable stock, hot

zest of 1 orange

Blanch the cauliflower florets in boiling water for 1 minute, drain, refresh under cold running water and dry in a cloth. Place in a bowl with the flour and spices and leave for 2 hours to allow the flavours to infuse.

Heat the oil in a heavy-based pan, add the cauliflower and spices and fry lightly together over a low heat for 5 minutes until golden on all sides. Add the onion and garlic and cook for a further 2 minutes. Add the tomatoes, dates and vegetable stock and simmer for 15–20 minutes. Finally stir in the herbs and season to taste.

Meanwhile, for the pilaff, heat the oil in a pan, add the almonds and cook for 5–6 minutes until golden. Remove them, add the onion and currants to the oil and cook for 2 minutes. Add the cinnamon and cook for a further 30 seconds. Add the rice and coat with the onions and cinnamon. Pour over the hot stock, cover and cook over a low heat for 15 minutes. Remove from the heat and leave, covered, for a further 5 minutes. Stir in the orange zest and almonds, adjust the seasoning and serve alongside the tagine.

Swiss chard and sweetcorn crespelle
with goat's cheese

Crespelle is the Italian name for these delicate, yet simple, light pancakes flavoured with sweetcorn, filled with a creamy chard and nut filling and baked in the oven until slightly crispy. The pancakes can be made a day in advance, then kept wrapped in clingfilm. To reheat, wrap them in tinfoil and place in the oven at 190°C/375°F/gas mark 5 for 10–15 minutes.

150g plain flour

2 free-range eggs

125ml full-fat milk

200g tinned sweetcorn, drained

1 tablespoon olive oil (plus some extra for cooking the pancakes)

1 red onion, chopped

350g Swiss chard, stalks discarded, chopped

2 tablespoons balsamic vinegar

200g goat's cheese

75g pine nuts

2 tablespoons chopped fresh mint

salt and freshly ground black pepper

Sift the flour into a bowl, add the eggs and milk and mix together. Place half the sweetcorn in a food processor, pour on the egg mixture and blend to a batter. Chop the remaining sweetcorn. Transfer the batter to a bowl, add the chopped sweetcorn and set aside for 30 minutes. The consistency should be that of single cream so add a little more milk if necessary.

Preheat the oven to 180°C/350°F/gas mark 4. Heat the olive oil in a large frying pan, add the onion and sauté over a low heat until golden. Add the chopped chard and cook for 4–5 minutes. Pour over the vinegar, add half the goat's cheese, the pine nuts and mint. Season to taste and keep warm.

Heat a little olive oil in a 15cm non-stick frying pan over a moderate heat. Fill a 50ml ladle or large spoon with batter and pour into the pan, tilting it so that the batter covers the base. Cook until pale golden or until the mixture begins to bubble. Turn it over and cook on the other side. Continue the process until all the batter is used up. You will need twelve crespelle in total. Fill each crespelle with the chard mixture and fold in half, flattening them lightly. Place in a well buttered gratin dish (using about 15g butter). Smear over the remaining goat's cheese and place in the oven until golden and slightly crispy. Serve immediately.

Grill-baked summer vegetables
with salsa all'agresto

The height of summer is the time to enjoy these twice-cooked vegetables. Salsa all'agresto is an Italian sauce which dates back to the Middle Ages. Similar in make-up to pesto, made with nuts, oil and herbs, but with the addition of verjuice (or unripened grape juice), it provides an intriguing flavour that gives us a glimpse of what people ate hundreds of years ago. If you can't find verjuice, try a mix of white wine vinegar, lemon juice and a little sugar. Serve with crusty bread to mop up the juices.

4 tablespoons extra-virgin olive oil

4 small aubergines, halved

4 plum tomatoes, halved

2 large courgettes, cut into thick wedges

12 asparagus tips, peeled and trimmed

1 garlic clove, crushed

for the salsa all'agresto

30g almonds

2 garlic cloves, crushed

good pinch of sugar

100g mixed herbs (flat-leaf parsley and basil)

125ml olive oil

90ml verjuice

salt and freshly ground black pepper

Preheat the oven to 220°C/425°F/gas mark 7. Heat a ridged grill pan until hot and then brush all over with a little olive oil. Add the vegetables and grill for 6–8 minutes on each side until soft and slightly charred. Remove the vegetables and place in a well oiled gratin dish.

For the salsa all'agresto, place the almonds, garlic, sugar and herbs in a food processor and blend until roughly chopped. With the motor running, add the oil in a thin stream through the funnel at the top, then do the same with the verjuice. Season. Spoon the salsa over the vegetables, cover the dish with tinfoil and bake for 5 minutes, then remove the tinfoil and cook for a further 2–3 minutes until lightly golden.

PG TIPS   For a lovely variation, mix in some buffalo mozzarella with the vegetables before covering with the salsa all'agresto.

Vegetable stifado
with spinach and tomato keftedes

A rich vegetable stew, based on a traditional Greek recipe made with morsels of beef. This vegetarian variety can be made in advance and reheated when needed. I recommend a large basket of crusty bread to mop up any remaining juices.

4 tablespoons olive oil

200g button onions

2 garlic cloves, crushed

1 teaspoon ground cumin

1 medium-sized cauliflower, cut into florets

2 large carrots, peeled and cut into thick slices

150g new potatoes, peeled and halved

1 tablespoon plain flour

200ml red wine

750ml good vegetable stock

100g sunblush tomatoes in oil, drained

175g cooked haricot beans

sprig of rosemary

12 black olives

2 tablespoons chopped fresh flat-leaf parsley

1 teaspoon chopped fresh oregano

salt and freshly ground black pepper

for the keftedes

4 ripe plum tomatoes, deseeded and chopped

100g cooked spinach, chopped

2 spring onions, finely chopped

1/2 teaspoon sugar

3 tablespoons self-raising flour

olive oil

salt and freshly ground black pepper

Preheat the oven to 190°C/375°F/gas mark 5. Heat half the oil in an ovenproof casserole over a moderate heat, add the button onions and cook for about 4–5 minutes until lightly golden. Add the garlic and cook for a further 1 minute. Add the cumin, cauliflower florets, carrots and potatoes and toss well together. Add the flour, stir well and cook for a further 1 minute. Add the red wine and stock, bring to the boil and add the tomatoes, cooked beans and rosemary. Place in the oven for 35–45 minutes until tender. When cooked, remove from the oven and stir in the remaining olive oil, then add the olives, parsley and oregano. Adjust the seasoning and keep hot (or cool if reheating later).

For the keftedes, place the tomatoes, spinach, spring onions and sugar in a bowl and season to taste. Add flour until the mixture is thick but still moist. Heat a little olive oil in a large non-stick frying pan and, when hot, drop spoonfuls of the tomato and spinach mixture into the oil, then fry on both sides for 2–3 minutes until golden. Drain on kitchen paper to remove excess grease and serve alongside the stifado.

Baked open cap mushrooms
with paneer and cumin spinach

The rise of Indian food over the last five years has been amazing, with good-quality, highly rated restaurants springing up all over the country. The cuisine has really been transformed by talented young Indian chefs who have taken it to new heights, replacing the staid curry houses of years ago. Here is a dish using paneer, an Indian curd cheese, now available from leading stores and Indian delicatessens.

8 large open cap mushrooms

4 tablespoons vegetable oil

175g paneer cheese, cut into 1cm dice

1/2 teaspoon coriander seeds

1cm piece of root ginger, peeled and finely chopped

1 small onion, finely chopped

1 small green chilli, deseeded and chopped

6 firm but ripe tomatoes

1 teaspoon tomato purée

pinch of saffron

1/2 teaspoon chilli powder

1 teaspoon fenugreek seeds

1 teaspoon garam masala

1 tablespoon honey

50g chopped fresh coriander

for the cumin spinach

1/2 teaspoon cumin seeds

1 garlic clove, crushed

450g fresh spinach, washed

salt and freshly ground black pepper

375g cooked basmati rice

Preheat the oven to 180°C/350°F/gas mark 4. Remove and roughly dice the stems from the mushrooms. Heat 3 tablespoons of oil in a large frying pan, add the mushrooms and cook for 3–4 minutes until golden. Remove and leave to cool. Add the paneer in two batches to the oil, fry until brown all over and set aside.

Heat the remaining oil in another frying pan and add the mushroom stems and cook for 2–3 minutes. Add the coriander seeds, ginger, onion and chilli and cook for 3–4 minutes or until softened and golden. Add the tomatoes, tomato purée and saffron and cook for a further 5 minutes. Add the remaining spices and honey. Transfer the paneer and half the coriander to the sauce.

Place the mushrooms in the base of a lightly greased ovenproof or baking dish. Fill each mushroom with the paneer mixture, then transfer the dish to the oven to bake for 6–8 minutes.

For the spinach, heat a frying pan over a moderate heat, add the cumin seeds and dry-fry for 30 seconds. Add the garlic and washed spinach and cook over a high heat until the spinach has wilted and any water evaporated. Season to taste.

Serve the stuffed baked mushrooms with the spinach and some basmati rice, sprinkle over the remaining coriander and serve.

Saag kebobs
with tomato and banana pickle and coconut yogurt

Throughout the subcontinent different religions impose food taboos that are rigidly adhered to. Many Indians are strict vegetarians, enjoying a cuisine that is in a class of its own and could convert even the most dedicated meat lover. These Indian-style spinach (saag) fritters are delicious. Make them smaller in size to serve as an appetiser.

for the tomato and banana pickle

2 tablespoons vegetable oil

1 teaspoon ground cumin

1 teaspoon ground cardamom

1 tablespoon mustard seeds

3 garlic cloves, crushed

1 teaspoon ground turmeric

1/2 teaspoon cayenne pepper

400g ripe but firm tomatoes, chopped

2 tablespoons malt vinegar

1 tablespoon caster sugar

2 bananas, peeled and cut into small dice

2cm piece of ginger, peeled and grated

for the coconut yogurt

100ml natural yogurt

50g freshly grated coconut (or desiccated is fine)

30g chopped fresh mint

for the spinach fritters

90g semolina

120g fresh spinach, picked and chopped

1 green chilli, deseeded

3 tablespoons cumin seeds, lightly toasted

good pinch of bicarbonate soda

1 tablespoon lemon juice

vegetable oil for deep-frying

small fresh mint leaves

salt and freshly ground black pepper

Prepare the pickle a day or two in advance. Heat the oil in a pan and add the cumin, cardamom, mustard seeds and garlic. Cook over a low heat until the garlic starts to brown. Add the turmeric, cayenne and chopped tomatoes, stir and cook for 2 minutes. Add the vinegar, sugar, bananas and ginger and simmer for about 10–15 minutes until thickened. Leave to cool then refrigerate, covered, until needed.

For the coconut yogurt, simply mix the ingredients together.

For the fritters, blend all the ingredients (except the oil and mint) in a food processor with approximately 80–100ml cold water to form a thick batter, then leave to stand for 30 minutes before use.

Heat the vegetable oil to 160ºC/325ºF. When ready, drop dessertspoonfuls of the mixture into the hot oil and deep-fry for 1–2 minutes until crisp and golden. Remove with a slotted spoon and place on kitchen paper to drain.

Place equal amounts of fritter on four serving plates with some tomato and banana pickle, drizzle with a little yogurt and serve some separately on the side. Scatter over the mint leaves and serve.

Kerala pumpkin curry
with cinnamon rice and beetroot raita

Curry leaves are small shiny flat leaves very similar in appearance to bay leaves. They are delicate and wonderfully flavoured, and can be found in Indian stores – well worth sourcing. The beetroot-flavoured raita makes not only a wonderful accompaniment, but finishes off a stunningly colourful dish.

2 tablespoons sunflower oil

1 large onion, chopped

5cm piece of root ginger, peeled and chopped

3 garlic cloves, crushed

$^1/_2$ teaspoon cumin seeds, lightly crushed

1 teaspoon good turmeric

$^1/_2$ teaspoon chilli powder

425g pumpkin, peeled, deseeded and cut into large pieces

150ml coconut milk

1 teaspoon mustard seeds

2 green chillies, chopped

8 curry leaves

200ml natural yogurt

for the beetroot raita

125ml natural yogurt

$^1/_2$ teaspoon salt

$^1/_2$ teaspoon sugar

pinch of ground cumin

2 medium-sized beetroots, cooked (see page 77), peeled and cut into 1cm dice

2 tablespoons chopped fresh mint

450g basmati rice, scented with cinnamon (see PG TIPS)

Heat half the oil in a heavy-based pan, add the onion and cook over a low heat for 8–10 minutes until soft. Meanwhile, blend the ginger and garlic to a paste together in a small food processor (or a pestle and mortar if you prefer). Add the paste to the onion and cook for 2–3 minutes. Add the cumin seeds, turmeric and chilli powder and cook for a further 1 minute. Throw in the pumpkin, mix well with the spices, add the coconut milk and simmer for about 15 minutes until cooked. (Do not let the pumpkin cook too much or it will go mushy.)

For the raita, place the yogurt in a bowl, add the salt, sugar and cumin, stir in the beetroot and chopped mint.

Heat a small frying pan with the remaining oil, throw in the mustard seeds, chillies and curry leaves and cook for 30 seconds until the seeds begin to pop. Add to the pumpkin curry, along with the yogurt and heat through for 2 minutes. Serve with the cinnamon-scented rice and beetroot raita.

PG TIPS For a fragrant sweet-tasting rice to accompany the curry, simply cook the rice as normal, but with the addition of some broken cinnamon in with the water. Remove before serving.

Black bean piperade
with melted cheddar and mint mojo verde

This is a great brunch or substantial lunch dish. A piperade is an egg dish flavoured with ratatouille-style vegetables, a speciality of southern France. In this recipe, I take the dish to Mexico for a spicier variation on the theme with a Cuban mojo salsa. Both the vegetables and the spicy green mojo sauce are all the better made in advance, allowing their flavours to develop. I suggest some country-style bread to serve with the piperades.

for the mint mojo verde

2 garlic cloves, peeled

20g fresh coriander leaves

40g fresh mint leaves

1 green pepper, deseeded and chopped

1 small green chilli, chopped

25g fresh white breadcrumbs

3 tablespoons olive oil

1 tablespoon white wine vinegar

4 tablespoons olive oil

1 onion, finely chopped

1 garlic clove, crushed

1 green chilli, deseeded and finely chopped

1/2 yellow pepper, deseeded and cut into 1cm dice

1/2 red pepper, deseeded and cut into 1cm dice

1 courgette, cut into 1cm dice

75g cooked Mexican black beans (tinned are fine)

1 tablespoon tomato purée

8 free-range eggs, separated

olive oil

75g freshly grated vegetarian cheddar cheese

salt and freshly ground black pepper

For the mint mojo verde, place the garlic, coriander, mint, pepper and green chilli in a small food processor and blend until finely chopped. Add the breadcrumbs, oil and vinegar, and blend again, scraping down the sides to ensure it is thoroughly mixed – the mojo should be a thick sauce. Set aside.

Heat half the olive oil in a large frying pan, add the onion, garlic and chilli and cook over a moderate heat until softened and tender. Add all the vegetables and the beans and cook for 2–3 minutes. Add the tomato purée and 2 tablespoons of water and mix well with the vegetables. Lower the heat, cover the pan with a lid and cook for 10–15 minutes until the vegetables are tender. Season to taste and leave to cool. Refrigerate if making in advance.

To make the piperade, whisk the egg whites until stiff, then add to the yolks. Incorporate together and season.

Divide the vegetables into four equal amounts and the egg mixture into four amounts. Heat each portion of vegetables in a little olive oil in a non-stick omelette pan or small frying pan. When hot, add the egg mixture and stir well together. Cook over a low heat until the piperade has a mousse-like consistency. Slide out the piperade onto a serving plate or shallow bowl, top with some of the cheddar and spoon on the mint mojo sauce. Cook one or two at at a time and keep warm while preparing the rest in the same way.

Vegetarian pho

Another delectable, Asian-style, heart-warming broth, this time heralding from Vietnam. Traditionally made with meat and fish, this vegetarian version is seasoned with vegetarian fish sauce – don't fear, this one is made of chillies, water, leeks, vinegar and sugar. You should ask for it at your oriental grocers. A smaller version can be served as an appetiser.

for the base broth

2 litres good vegetable stock

2 tablespoons soy sauce

6 garlic cloves, crushed

1 onion, chopped

2cm piece of root ginger, peeled and grated

1 stick of cinnamon

2 star anise

1 bay leaf

2 sticks of celery, thinly sliced

4 spring onions, finely shredded

2 carrots, finely shredded

200g Chinese cabbage, finely shredded

75g beansprouts

1 teaspoon vegetarian fish sauce (nuoc mam chay)

2 tablespoons soy sauce

350g buckwheat 'soba' noodles

20 fresh basil leaves

100g fresh coriander

1 red chilli, thinly sliced

1 lime, cut into wedges

salt and freshly ground black pepper

For the broth, place the stock, soy sauce, garlic and onion in a pan and bring to the boil. Add the ginger, cinnamon stick, star anise and bay leaf. Reduce the heat to a simmer and cook for 20 minutes. Strain the broth and replace on the heat.

Add all the vegetables, vegetarian fish sauce and soy sauce and cook for 10 minutes. Add the noodles and simmer for a further 5 minutes. Season. Pour into four large serving bowls, top with the herbs and chilli, squeeze over the lime juice and serve.

Funghi and grilled vegetable moussaka
with red ricotta glaze

Moussaka is a staple served in tavernas and prepared in homes throughout Greece. The wild mushrooms add a touch of elegance and the grilled vegetables a light smoky flavour that works so well when paired together. A fresh well dressed green salad makes a great accompaniment.

400g potatoes, peeled and cut into 1cm thick slices

3 aubergines, cut into 1cm thick slices

3 red peppers, halved, deseeded and cut into large pieces

2 courgettes, cut into 1cm thick slices

2 tablespoons extra-virgin olive oil

1 onion, finely chopped

2 garlic cloves, crushed

2 tablespoons chopped fresh oregano

20g dried wild mushrooms, soaked in a little red wine
    and drained

50g raisins

400g tin plum tomatoes, drained

1 tablespoon tomato purée

salt and freshly ground black pepper

for the red ricotta glaze

2 free-range egg yolks

1 garlic clove, crushed

300ml passata

150g ricotta cheese

100ml double cream

salt and freshly ground black pepper

1-litre ovenproof casserole dish

Heat a ridged grill pan and, when smoking, brush the potatoes, aubergines, peppers and courgettes with a little olive oil, then grill for 8–10 minutes until tender and lightly charred all over. Season well and set aside.

Heat the remaining olive oil in a pan, add the onion, garlic, oregano, mushrooms and raisins and cook over a moderate heat for 4–5 minutes before adding the chopped tomatoes and tomato purée. Cook for 10–15 minutes until the sauce becomes thick with very little sauce left.

Preheat the oven to 160°C/325°F/gas mark 3. Lightly grease the casserole dish. Pour the wild mushroom sauce into the base of the dish, then arrange overlapping slices of the grilled vegetables over the surface, with an eye for colour.

For the glaze, beat the egg yolks, garlic, passata and ricotta in a bowl. Pour in the cream and season well. Pour the egg mixture over the vegetables, ensuring all the vegetables are covered. Place in the oven to bake for 20 minutes, or until the top is golden brown. Remove from the oven and allow to sit for 2–3 minutes before cutting into portions to serve.

Green jungle curry

with lychees, green peppers and coconut rice cakes

Unlike most versions that generally contain coconut milk, this Thai curry is thin in appearance, full of vegetables and quite spicy. Originally jungle curries were made of wild boar, but nowadays they are more likely to be made with chicken or pork. This vegetarian version is wonderful.

for the rice cakes

250ml coconut milk

1 teaspoon ground turmeric

200g Thai jasmine rice

1 free-range egg yolk

30g unsalted butter

2 tablespoons vegetable oil

2 shallots, thinly sliced

2cm piece of root ginger, peeled and finely chopped

2 sticks of lemongrass, outer casing discarded,
  finely chopped

1/2 teaspoon fennel seeds, crushed

1 heaped tablespoon Thai green curry paste

200g sugar snap peas

150g baby sweetcorn

100g French beans, trimmed

1 large turnip, peeled and cut into 1cm dice

75g Thai pea aubergines

8 asparagus tips

900ml good vegetable stock

10 Thai basil leaves

4 kaffir lime leaves, shredded

1 teaspoon green peppercorns

1 small tin lychees, drained

20 x 30cm baking/cake tin

For the rice cakes, put 250ml water, the coconut milk and turmeric in a pan and bring to the boil. Add the rice and simmer gently for 10–15 minutes until cooked and all the liquid has gone. Mix in the egg yolk, then remove to a greased baking tin or cake tin, spread over with a palette knife to ensure the top is smooth. Refrigerate to set overnight.

For the curry, heat the oil in a pan, add the shallots, ginger, lemongrass and fennel seeds and cook for 1 minute. Add the Thai curry paste and stir together to infuse the flavours. Add the vegetables, toss with the spices, then add the vegetable stock and bring to the boil. Add the Thai basil, kaffir lime leaves and peppercorns and reduce to a simmer. Cook gently for 10–12 minutes or until the vegetables are tender. Add the lychees and heat through.

Take the rice from the fridge, remove from the tin and cut the slab into neat 5cm square cakes. Fry in the butter for 1–2 minutes on each side until crisp.

Serve the curry into four serving bowls and garnish each with a small pile of fried coconut rice cakes.

Aubergine and mozzarella croquettes
with sherry-glazed vegetables

The use of Japanese-style breadcrumbs called panko to coat the aubergine rolls gives this dish a real crispiness when fried. By adding honey to them they obtain a wonderful golden colour, an idea I learnt from a great chef and friend, Peter Gordon. Panko are available from oriental stores, although fresh white breadcrumbs can be used instead. I often serve this dish with garlic mayonnaise (aioli – see PG TIPS page 102) to be passed around the table.

2 medium-sized aubergines, stalks removed

120ml olive oil

180g mozzarella, thinly sliced

100g sunblush tomatoes, drained and chopped

3 tablespoons plain flour

2 free-range eggs, lightly beaten

150g panko crumbs (mixed with 2 tablespoons honey)

vegetable oil for deep-frying

for the vegetables

2 red peppers, deseeded and cut into thick strips

2 yellow peppers, deseeded and cut into thick strips

1 red onion, cut into large dice

2 garlic cloves, halved

50g black olives

4 small baby courgettes, cut into slices on bias

1 teaspoon light brown sugar

100ml dry sherry

4 sprigs of rosemary

3 tablespoons olive oil

salt and freshly ground black pepper

toothpicks

Preheat the oven to 200°C/400°F/gas mark 6. Using a large knife, cut the aubergine lengthways into 1cm-thick slices. Heat the olive oil in a large frying pan. When hot add the aubergine slices a few at a time and cook for 2–3 minutes on each side until golden. Remove with a slotted spoon onto kitchen paper to drain and cool.

Place twelve cooked slices onto a work surface, divide the mozzarella and top the aubergine with it. Place a spoonful of chopped tomatoes on top and carefully roll them up tightly. Secure with a toothpick, then dust all over with flour. Pass through the beaten egg, then coat in the honey-coated panko crumbs. Brush off any excess crumbs, place on a plate and refrigerate.

For the vegetables, place the peppers, onion, garlic, olives and courgettes in a large roasting tin. Sprinkle over the sugar, pour over the sherry and season with a little salt and pepper. Cover the tin with tinfoil and bake for 40 minutes. Remove the tinfoil, add the rosemary and olive oil and return to the oven, uncovered, for a further 10 minutes until the vegetables are tender.

Meanwhile, heat the vegetable oil in a frying pan or large pan. When hot (approximately 160°C/325°F), carefully immerse half the aubergine croquettes and cook for about 2–3 minutes until golden and crisp. Remove with a slotted spoon and drain on kitchen paper. Cook the remainder in the same way. Arrange the croquettes on a bed of the sherry-glazed vegetables on four serving plates and serve.

PG TIPS   These sherry-glazed vegetables are wonderful served just on their own, topped with grated feta and crispy bread as an appetiser.

Bombay tortillas
with spiced squash, peas and coconut yogurt

A real East-meets-West dish here. Mexican flour tortillas – a staple of
Mexican eating – form a wrap for a spiced squash and pea filling and are
then baked under a thin veil of yogurt and mild cheese.

2 tablespoons ghee or unsalted butter

1 onion, chopped

1 poblano chilli, roasted (see PG TIPS)

325g butternut squash or pumpkin, peeled and cut into
    2cm dice

200g tinned plum tomatoes, chopped

100g sunblush tomatoes

1 teaspoon cumin seeds

1/2 teaspoon ground coriander

100g fresh or frozen peas

8 flour tortillas

2 tablespoons chopped fresh coriander

coconut yogurt (see page 135)

100g freshly grated vegetarian mild cheddar cheese

Preheat the oven to 200°C/400°F/gas mark 6. In a large frying pan, heat the ghee or butter, add the onion and cook for 2–3 minutes. Shred the roasted poblano chilli, add to the pan and cook for a further 2 minutes. Add the squash and cook for 15–20 minutes over a moderate heat. Add both types of tomato, cumin seeds, ground coriander and peas, then reduce the heat and cook for 5 minutes to infuse the flavours and form a sauce.

Lay out the flour tortillas on a work surface, fill with the squash mixture, then roll them up tightly to secure the filling. Place them in a large well buttered (using about 15g butter) ovenproof gratin dish, then spoon over the yogurt and sprinkle with chopped coriander. Liberally scatter over the cheese, then transfer to the oven to heat through for about 8–10 minutes before serving.

PG TIPS   Roasting chillies like the Mexicans do really brings out their flavour. To roast them, simply place them directly over a gas flame and leave for 2–3 minutes, turning them occasionally until blistered and black in colour. Alternatively place under a hot preheated grill until charred, turning them regularly. When charred, place in a small plastic kitchen bag and seal it tightly to allow the chillies to steam for 5 minutes and loosen their skins. Peel off their skins, half them, then remove the inner seeds and use as required.

Bubble and squeak frittata

with crumbled feta and olives

For this dish be sure to use good firm waxy potatoes, like Charlottes or Juliettes, which are not only great tasting, but hold their shape during cooking too. This is a great lunch dish served with a simple salad or for a hearty brunch or breakfast treat. Make this recipe as one large dish or four smaller individual ones.

400g waxy potatoes, peeled and cut into small 1cm dice

175g savoy cabbage, leaves chopped

12 free-range eggs

150ml full-fat milk

1 teaspoon chopped fresh rosemary (plus a little for garnishing)

25g unsalted butter

2 tablespoons olive oil

1/2 garlic clove, crushed

100g Greek feta cheese, crumbled

12 black olives, stoned and roughly chopped

salt and freshly ground black pepper

Preheat the oven to 180°C/350°F/gas mark 4. Cook the potatoes and cabbage in separate pans of boiling water for 20–25 minutes until just cooked, then drain them well and dry them both.

Beat the eggs and milk in a bowl with the rosemary and a little salt and pepper.

Place a heavy-based frying pan over a moderate heat and add the butter and olive oil. Add the cooked potatoes and cabbage and the garlic, stir together well in the oil and butter and cook for 6–8 minutes. Pour over the egg mixture and cook until it begins to set at the edges. Using a fork, draw the edges into the middle, allowing the edges to set again. Sprinkle over the feta and olives, transfer to the oven and cook for 7–10 minutes or until firm. Slide onto a plate, garnish with rosemary and serve.

Baked peppers
with chickpea and apricot pilau and smoked almond dukkah

An excellent dish packed full of energy and flavour with its roots in the Middle East. The use of smoked almonds for the dukkah – a spiced seasoning popular in Egypt – adds a wonderful smoky overtone to the dish. I suggest serving the peppers on a bed of buttered garlic spinach and roasted squash.

400ml good vegetable stock

good pinch of saffron

175g brown rice

6 tablespoons olive oil

50g pine nuts

1 onion, finely chopped

1/2 teaspoon ground coriander

1/2 teaspoon ground cumin

120g cooked chickpeas (tinned are fine), drained

50g raisins

40g dried apricots, soaked in water, drained
 and chopped

1 tablespoon flat-leaf parsley, chopped

4 large red peppers, halved and deseeded, stalks intact

4 tablespoons balsamic vinegar

2 tablespoons honey

salt and freshly ground black pepper

smoked almond dukkah

25g smoked almonds

20g sesame seeds

15g coriander seeds

1/2 teaspoon cumin seeds

little salt and freshly cracked black pepper

Preheat the oven to 220°C/400°F/gas mark 6. Gently heat the vegetable stock in a pan and infuse the saffron in it for 4–5 minutes. Add the rice and simmer, covered, for 20–25 minutes or until the rice is tender and all the stock has been absorbed.

Heat 3 tablespoons of the oil in a large non-stick frying pan, add the pine nuts and cook over a low heat until golden; remove and set aside. Heat the remaining 3 tablespoons of oil in the pan, add the onion and cook until lightly golden. Add the ground coriander, cumin, chickpeas, raisins and apricots and cook for 1 minute. Stir in the rice, add the chopped parsley and season to taste. Fill the pepper halves with the prepared pilau and place in a large roasting tin. Mix together the vinegar, honey and 100ml water, then pour the liquid into the base of the roasting tin. Place the tin in the oven and cook for 35–40 minutes.

For the smoked almond dukkah, heat a dry frying pan and, when hot, add the almonds and seeds and toast for 30 seconds, stirring all the time. Transfer to a mortar and crush with a pestle, but not too finely, and season.

When the peppers are cooked, remove to four serving plates, sprinkle liberally with the dukkah, whisk the pan cooking juices and pour over the peppers.

PG TIPS   The dukkah can be made in advance and kept in a sealed container. It is great sprinkled on salads and over fried eggs. It is also becoming increasingly popular as a dry-spice dip for olive oil-drenched slices of bread in restaurants.

Butternut squash and blue cheese tacos
with white truffle oil

The slightly sweet-tasting squash is complemented here by the sharp blue cheese, making an interesting combination. White truffle oil is becoming a more common ingredient now, as it gives a good perfume to foods, but at a fraction of the cost of fresh truffles. A grill pan will do fine, but for the best results use a charcoal grill.

4 tablespoons olive oil (plus more for coating)

300g butternut squash (or other winter squash),
   peeled and cut into 1cm dice

1 garlic clove, crushed

100g tinned sweetcorn, well drained

1 small onion, finely chopped

100g roquefort (or other blue cheese)

1 teaspoon fresh thyme leaves

8 x 15cm corn tortillas

2 tablespoons white truffle oil

salt and freshly ground black pepper

Heat the olive oil in a large frying pan over a moderate heat, add the squash, garlic, sweetcorn and onion and cook for 8–10 minutes until golden and just tender when pierced with a knife. Remove to a bowl, add the roquefort and thyme and lightly mash with a fork. Season to taste and leave to cool.

Place the tortillas on a flat surface, fill the centre of each with the cheese mixture, then fold each tortilla in half over the filling to make a semi-circle. Brush the tops lightly with olive oil. Place on a preheated charcoal grill or hot grill pan and grill for about 2–3 minutes until golden brown. Brush with olive oil, turn over and grill on the other side. Drizzle with the truffle oil and serve.

Persian ratatouille-baked tomatoes
with cashew kibbeh crust

Stuffed vegetables are popular all over the Middle East and date back to ancient times. They are served with a variety of sweet and sour sauces, ranging from spiced syrups of lime to tamarind and butter. The tomatoes can be prepared a day in advance and baked when needed. They are also delicious served cold with warm flatbread.

for the tomatoes

4 tablespoons olive oil

1 onion, chopped

2 garlic cloves, crushed

1 aubergine, cut into 1cm dice

1 courgette, cut into 1cm dice

2 green peppers, deseeded and cut into 1cm dice

175g young leeks, cut into 1cm lengths

1 tablespoon tomato purée

1 tablespoon sugar

50g raisins

1 teaspoon orange zest

3 tablespoons chopped fresh coriander

8 beef tomatoes, tops discarded and
   seeds scooped out

salt and freshly ground black pepper

for the syrup

175ml white wine vinegar

4 tablespoons golden syrup

good pinch of saffron

50g unsalted butter

salt and freshly ground black pepper

for the cashew kibbeh crust

100g bulghur, soaked in warm water for 10 minutes

100g cashew nuts

1/2 teaspoon ground cinnamon

1/2 teaspoon ground cumin

pinch of cayenne pepper

little olive oil

Preheat the oven to 160°C/325°F/gas mark 3. For the ratatouille, heat half the olive oil in a large pan over a moderate heat, add the onion and garlic and cook for 2–3 minutes until softened. Add the vegetables, stir well and cook for 5–6 minutes until they begin to soften. Add the tomato purée, sugar, raisins and orange zest and stir well. Pour over the remaining oil, cover, reduce the heat and cook for 20 minutes. Remove and cool slightly before adding the coriander.

Meanwhile, for the basting syrup, boil together the vinegar, golden syrup and saffron, then whisk in the butter, season and set aside.

Fill the beef tomatoes with the ratatouille and place in a baking dish. Drizzle the prepared syrup over and around the tomatoes.

For the kibbeh crust, place the cracked wheat, cashew nuts, spices and olive oil in a food processor and blend together.

Sprinkle the mixture over the tomatoes and bake in the oven for 20 minutes until golden. Allow to cool slightly before serving.

Greek-stuffed onions

with feta cheese custard

A type of modern-day vegetarian moussaka, these sweet oven-roasted onions are filled with a herby tomato, nut and mushroom filling, then baked inside a rich feta cheese custard. I like to serve these onions with some well-made pilaff-style rice and a crispy green leaf salad.

8 medium-sized red onions, unpeeled

3 tablespoons olive oil

25g unsalted butter

1 onion, finely chopped

1 garlic clove, crushed

25g pack of dried porcini mushrooms, soaked in water
   for 30 minutes and drained

75g sunblush tomatoes in oil, drained and chopped

2 tablespoons chopped fresh flat-leaf parsley

1 tablespoon chopped fresh oregano
   (or $1/2$ teaspoon dried)

120g fresh white breadcrumbs

50g cashew nuts, chopped

pinch of cinnamon

1 free-range egg, lightly beaten

50g feta cheese, grated

salt and freshly ground black pepper

for the feta cheese custard

15g unsalted butter

15g plain flour

300ml full-fat milk

300ml single cream

120g finely grated feta cheese

2 free-range eggs, lightly beaten

salt and freshly ground black pepper

Preheat the oven to 200°C/400°F/gas mark 6. Remove a good slice off the top of each onion, then place in a baking tin or ovenproof dish. Spoon a little water over each onion, then drizzle over some of the olive oil. Cover the dish with tinfoil and bake for 1 hour or until the onions are tender. Remove them, leave to cool and peel.

For the stuffing, heat the remaining oil and butter in a large frying pan, add the onion and garlic and cook until softened and beginning to brown. Add the soaked porcini, cook for 2–3 minutes, then add the tomatoes and herbs. Finally, add the breadcrumbs, cashew nuts and cinnamon. Cook for a further 1 minute and then transfer to a bowl. Add the beaten egg and cheese, stir until thoroughly combined and season to taste.

Carefully remove the centres from each cooked onion. Chop the centre and add to the stuffing mixture. Fill each onion generously with the stuffing, then place in a suitable-sized baking dish, leaving at least 1–2cm gap between them.

To prepare the custard, place the butter, flour and milk into a pan. Heat gently, whisking constantly until the sauce thickens and becomes glossy and smooth. Reduce the heat, simmer for 1–2 minutes, then remove and cool slightly. Add the cream and grated feta, beat in the eggs and season to taste. Pour the cheese custard carefully between the onions, then return the dish to the oven to bake for 20–25 minutes. Allow to cool slightly before serving.

Fennel and courgette osso bucco
with castelli gremolata and saffron couscous

For me, fennel is one of the most underrated and underutilised vegetables there are. Usually partnered with fish, it makes great vegetarian dishes and this is one of my favourite ways to cook it.

90ml olive oil

1 onion, finely chopped

1 garlic clove, crushed

$1/2$ teaspoon fennel seed

4 heads of fennel, halved lengthways, fronds removed

2 courgettes, cut into 5cm thick slices on bias

400g tinned tomatoes, chopped

100g sunblush tomatoes, chopped

1 teaspoon tomato purée

5 tablespoons orange juice

700ml good vegetable stock

12 black olives, stoned

70g raisins

30g pine nuts, toasted

2 tablespoons chopped fresh coriander

for the castelli gremolata

50g fresh white breadcrumbs

2 tablespoons freshly grated castelli vegetalia (parmesan-
    style cheese)

$1/2$ teaspoon grated lemon zest

$1/2$ garlic clove, crushed

40g unsalted butter, melted

salt and freshly ground black pepper

for the saffron couscous

200g couscous

250ml good vegetable stock

1 teaspoon saffron

salt and freshly ground black pepper

Preheat the oven to 200°C/400°F/gas mark 6. Heat the olive oil in a large frying pan, add the onion, garlic and fennel seed and cook until softened. Add the fennel and cook for 3–4 minutes until it takes on a little colour. Add the courgettes and cook for a further 2–3 minutes. Add the tinned tomatoes, sunblush tomatoes, tomato purée, orange juice and vegetable stock. Bring to the boil, add the olives, raisins and pine nuts and cook for 5–6 minutes. Transfer the fennel, courgettes and sauce to an ovenproof gratin dish.

For the castelli gremolata, combine the breadcrumbs, castelli vegetalia, lemon zest, garlic, butter and a little seasoning in a bowl. Sprinkle it evenly over the vegetables, then place in the oven until the top is crisp and golden.

For the saffron couscous, infuse the vegetable stock with the saffron for 2 minutes and then strain. Place the couscous in a bowl, pour over the hot vegetable stock, cover with clingfilm or a lid and leave for 5 minutes. Fork through the couscous, cover for a futher 2–3 minutes and then season to taste. Place the couscous on serving plates, top with the fennel and courgette osso bucco, scatter over the chopped coriander and serve.

Courgette linguine
with cashew pesto and marinated mushrooms and brocccoli

A refreshing variation of the classic pesto. Tossed with raw delicate threads of courgette, marinated mushrooms and crunchy broccoli, this is an outstanding plate of colour and texture.

for the cashew pesto

50g raw cashews

2 small garlic cloves, crushed

1 small red chilli, deseeded and finely chopped

2cm piece of root ginger, peeled and grated

100ml groundnut oil or extra-virgin olive oil

25g fresh coriander leaves

40g fresh mint leaves

juice of 1 lime

200g chestnut mushrooms

100ml extra-virgin olive oil

1 tablespoon shoyu (Japanese soy sauce)

2 garlic cloves, crushed

1 spring onion, finely chopped

2cm piece of root ginger, peeled and grated

100g broccoli, cut into florets

juice of 2 limes

4 crispy and firm courgettes

sea salt and freshly ground black pepper

For the cashew pesto, place the cashews in a blender and blitz until broken down. Add the garlic, chilli and ginger and blend to a paste. Add the oil and herbs and blend until puréed. Finish with the lime juice and sea salt. Set aside.

Slice the mushrooms very thinly, place in a bowl and add the oil, soy sauce, garlic, onion and ginger. Allow to marinate for 30 minutes or until soft.

Meanwhile, steam the broccoli until it turns bright green but is still crunchy in texture. Quickly remove and add to the mushrooms, along with the lime juice and season to taste. Cut off the ends of the courgettes, then slice, using a kitchen mandolin or knife, as thinly as possible lengthways into strips or 'linguine'. Toss with the mushroom and broccoli, adjust the seasoning and serve.

Grilled paneer cheese
with Indian bread salad

The inspiration for this light main course dish is based on a similar bread salad from Tuscany, called panzanella. I experimented on the idea of adding some Asian flavours on the same theme, and replaced the more usual bread for naan bread. The result was deemed worthy of inclusion, so here it is. These little kebabs taste even better if cooked on a charcoal grill. Indian paneer cheese is similar to Asian tofu in that it has a bland flavour in itself, but often absorbs the flavours of other ingredients well. It is ideal for grilling and roasting, and can be found in Asian food stores.

75g fresh mint, finely chopped

4 tablespoons natural yogurt

50g finely grated vegetarian mild cheddar cheese

2cm piece of root ginger, peeled and finely grated

2 garlic cloves, crushed

1/2 teaspoon cumin seeds, toasted

1/2 teaspoon marjoram, toasted

2 x 375g paneer cheese

little sunflower oil for cooking

salt and freshly ground black pepper

for the bread salad

6 tablespoons sunflower oil

juice of 2 lemons

1 red onion, cut into thin rings

2 red peppers, deseeded and chopped

350g firm but ripe tomatoes, chopped

2 naan bread, cut or torn into pieces

1 red chilli, finely chopped

1cm piece of root ginger, peeled and finely grated

50g fresh coriander, roughly torn

25g fresh mint, roughly torn

salt and freshly ground black pepper

large wooden bamboo skewers, soaked (see PG TIPS)

Mix together the mint, yogurt, grated cheddar and ginger in a bowl. Add the garlic, cumin, marjoram and a little seasoning to form a thick paste (adding a little more cheddar if necessary).

Cut the paneer into 8 x 5cm blocks, and then with a sharp small knife, cut down each cheese into three sections, without cutting right through the base, about 1cm from the bottom. Using a small palette knife, thickly smear the insides of all the cheeses with the paste, then skewer two blocks lengthways with a soaked skewer (or two) to secure them tightly while cooking.

For the bread salad, combine the oil, lemon juice and 2 tablespoons of water in a large bowl. Add the vegetables and toss well. Add the naan bread, chilli, ginger and herbs and mix well. Allow to stand for about 15 minutes for the flavours to meld and season to taste. Heat a ridged grill pan with a little oil. When hot, place the paneer skewers on it and grill for 3–4 minutes, turning them regularly, until lightly charred all over.

Share the salad between four serving plates or bowls. Remove the cheese from the grill, arrange on the salad and serve immediately.

PG TIPS Wooden skewers, when placed on a charcoal grill, have the tendency to burn and fall apart. To counteract this, simply soak the skewers in water for 24 hours and use on the grill without any worries.

Plantain empanadas
with mango and sweetcorn salsa and arroz verde

It is vitally important that the plantains are just ripe (yellow with black mottling), as overripe black plantains are too starchy to wrap the beans.

3 yellow-black mottled plantains (about 900g)

300g black beans

vegetable oil for cooking

1 onion, chopped

2 garlic cloves, crushed

1 green chilli, deseeded and finely chopped

1 green pepper, deseeded and finely chopped

1 teaspoon ground cumin

2 tablespoons honey

1 tablespoon white wine vinegar

125g feta cheese, crumbled

110g plain flour

fresh coriander leaves to garnish

120ml sour cream (optional)

salt and freshly ground black pepper

for the arroz verde (green rice)

1 small onion, finely chopped

1 green chilli, deseeded and quartered

3 garlic cloves, crushed

100g fresh coriander leaves

425ml good vegetable stock

2 tablespoons vegetable oil

200g long-grain white rice

for the mango and corn salsa

200g tinned sweetcorn, drained

1 mango, stoned and cut into 1cm dice

25g chopped fresh coriander

2 firm but ripe tomatoes, cut into 1cm dice

1 shallot, chopped

1 garlic clove, crushed

juice of 2 limes

2 tablespoons maple syrup

Preheat the oven to 220ºC/425ºF/gas mark 7. Using a small knife, cut a slit through the peel of each plantain from top to bottom along the inner curve, then place in a baking tin. Bake in the oven for up to 50 minutes. Leave to cool for 1 hour.

Cook the black beans in boiling salted water for 30–40 minutes and drain.

Heat a little vegetable oil in a frying pan, add the onion, garlic, chilli, green pepper and cumin and cook over a low heat until tender. Add the beans and cook for 5 minutes for the flavours to infuse, then add the honey and vinegar. Cook for a further 1 minute, transfer to a bowl and leave to cool. Mash the mixture finely with a potato masher and season to taste. Add the feta and set aside.

Peel the plantains, then blend in a food processor until they come together as dough. Remove, add the flour and roll the dough in lightly oiled hands into eight equal-sized balls. Roll out the dough balls with a rolling pin to about 1cm thick. Fill each of the rolled dough balls with a good spoonful of the black bean mixture and fold over carefully to form pasties, crimping the edges with your thumb and finger to seal. Prepare all the same way. Refrigerate until required.

For the green rice, place the onion, chilli, garlic, coriander and half of the stock in a food processor, blend well until smooth and season with a little salt and pepper. Heat the oil in a heavy-based pan and add the rice, stirring constantly for 1 minute. Add the green stock and the remaining vegetable stock, bring to the boil and simmer for 20 minutes. Remove the pan from the heat but keep covered, allowing the rice to steam for a further 5 minutes.

For the salsa, mix all the ingredients together in a bowl and season to taste.

Heat 5–7cm of vegetable oil in a deep-fat fryer or large pan to about 160ºC/325ºF, add the empanadas and fry for about 2–3 minutes until golden. Transfer to kitchen paper to drain. Serve the empanadas on a bed of the green rice, with the cool tasting salsa alongside and garnish with the coriander leaves and a good dollop of the sour cream, if desired.

Pastry

Who can resist a dish of any sort made with pastry? I know I can't! There is something so comforting about food encased in a light crisp, or rich buttery crust. The fillings can be as varied as your imagination and taste. Using pastry in vegetarian cooking is particularly successful – it not only gives focus to a dish, but also adds substance and the necessary protein needed for a balanced vegetarian diet.

Grated celeriac, camembert and prune tarts
with warm lentil vinaigrette

This lovely celeriac tart makes enough for four main courses or six as an appetiser. I discovered the flavoursome marriage of camembert cheeses and prunes at a recent promotion launch I prepared at the hotel last year.

300g prepared fresh shortcrust pastry

50g unsalted butter

1 small celeriac, peeled and coarsely grated

175ml crème fraîche (or double cream)

240g firm but ripe camembert, cut into 1cm dice

100g ready-to-eat prunes (stones removed), chopped

3 free-range eggs

1 free-range egg yolk

salt, freshly ground black pepper and ground nutmeg

for the lentil vinaigrette

250g puy lentils

2 garlic cloves, crushed

2 teaspoons Dijon mustard

2 tablespoons balsamic vinegar

6 tablespoons extra-virgin olive oil

1 small red onion, sliced

120g baby spinach leaves

50g watercress, tough stalks removed

salt and freshly cracked black pepper

25cm loose-bottomed tart tin

serves 4–6

Preheat the oven to 200°C/400°F/gas mark 6. Roll out the pastry to 1cm thick and use it to line a greased loose-bottomed tart tin. Prick with a fork all over and then chill for 20 minutes. Line the pastry bottom with baking paper and fill with baking beans. Bake blind for 20 minutes. Carefully remove the beans and paper, then return the tin to the oven to cook for a further 5 minutes. Remove and cool slightly.

Melt the butter in a pan, add the celeriac and cook over a gentle heat for 5 minutes. Pour in the crème fraîche and simmer for 10 minutes. Remove from the heat, add half the camembert, the prunes, stir in the eggs and mix well. Season with salt, pepper and nutmeg. Pour the mixture into the pastry case, dot with the remaining camembert and cook for 20 minutes or until firm to the touch. Remove from the oven and leave to cool.

Meanwhile for the lentils, place them in a pan, cover with water, bring to the boil and simmer for 20 minutes. Top up with more water if necessary.

In a bowl, whisk together the garlic, mustard, vinegar and olive oil. When the lentils are cooked, drain them thoroughly, then add the dressing and mix well. Add the remaining ingredients, toss together gently and season with salt and freshly cracked black pepper. Serve the tart, cut into wedges, with the warm lentil vinaigrette.

Goat's cheese and polenta tart
with caramelised onions and grilled vegetables

The goat's cheese and polenta filling is lovely served on its own, without the crisp pastry tarts. This dish is enjoyed by many vegetarian diners at The Lanesborough, where it has been a favourite for many years.

375g prepared shortcrust pastry

600ml milk or water

200g tinned sweetcorn, well drained

150g quick-cook polenta

30g unsalted butter

100g herb goat's cheese

4 tablespoons olive oil

2 red onions, thinly sliced

2 teaspoons caster sugar

2 tablespoons balsamic vinegar

4 baby courgettes, halved horizontally

2 portobello mushrooms, thickly sliced

4 plum tomatoes, halved

2 red peppers, halved, deseeded and cut into thick strips

2 garlic cloves, crushed

4 tablespoons basil pesto (bought or home-made – see PG TIPS page 103)

12 fresh basil leaves

salt and freshly ground black pepper

4 x 9cm-diameter tartlet tins or pastry rings

Preheat the oven to 190°C/375°F/gas mark 5. Roll out the pastry to 5mm thick to line the tartlet tins or pastry rings. Fill with a little baking paper and baking beans and bake blind for 10–12 minutes. Remove the baking beans and paper and return to the oven for a further 5 minutes. Remove and cool before removing the pastry cases from the tins. These tartlets can be prepared in advance.

Bring the milk or water to the boil, add the sweetcorn and cook for 5 minutes. Transfer to a food processor and blend to a smooth liquid. Return the corn milk to the pan, bring to the boil and stir in the polenta to a smooth paste. Reduce the heat and cook for 10–12 minutes, stirring frequently. Add the butter and goat's cheese and season to taste. Keep hot.

Heat the olive oil in a pan, add the onions and cook over a moderate heat for 5 minutes until softened. Add the sugar and vinegar and cook for a further 10–12 minutes, stirring occasionally until soft and caramelised. Set aside.

Place the vegetables in a bowl, add the garlic and remaining olive oil and toss together. Heat a ridged grill pan and, when hot, add the vegetables and grill, turning them regularly, until cooked and lightly caramelised.

Fill the cooked tartlets with some caramelised onions then top with the goat's cheese polenta, levelling off the surface with a wet palette knife. Top each tartlet with a heaped pile of grilled vegetables, drizzle the basil pesto over and around the tartlets. Garnish with fresh basil leaves and serve.

PG TIPS   For a tasty variation to this dish, why not top the vegetables with a slice or two of thin Tuscan scamorza – a soft, delicate cheese popular throughout Italy.

Torta di scalogni

A simple torta or Italian-style free-form pie made from candied shallots with raisins and delectable Italian taleggio cheese wrapped in a thin pastry, then baked until crispy. Ideally served hot from the oven, it's also good cold served with a crisp salad as part of an interesting picnic. If you don't have a pizza sheet, use a flat baking sheet and cut the dough to the right size.

for the dough

250g plain flour, plus little extra for dusting

1/2 teaspoon salt

3 tablespoons extra-virgin olive oil

for the filling

25g unsalted butter

425g small shallots, peeled

50g raisins

1 tablespoon caster sugar

1 tablespoon red wine vinegar

200ml roasted vegetable stock (see page 189)

175g taleggio cheese, cut into small dice

2 tablespoons walnuts, roughly chopped

1 tablespoon marjoram

33cm round pizza sheet

serves 6

Mix together the flour and salt in a large bowl and make a well in the centre. Add the oil and 100ml cold water a little at a time and bring in the sides. Carefully work the dough until it just holds together. Knead the dough until smooth and elastic, then shape into a ball and return to the bowl. Cover and refrigerate for up to 2 hours.

For the filling, heat the butter in a large non-stick pan and, when hot, add the shallots and raisins and roll them in the butter for 1 minute. Sprinkle over the sugar and lightly caramelise for 2–3 minutes. Add the vinegar and vegetable stock and bring to the boil. Cover and cook over a moderate heat for 15 minutes until the shallots are soft and the liquid all but evaporated. Tip into a bowl and leave to cool.

Preheat the oven to 180°C/350°F/gas mark 4. Lightly oil and flour a large 33cm-round pizza sheet. Split the dough in two and roll one piece to cover the pizza pan. Cut off any overhanging dough with a knife.

Add the taleggio, walnuts and marjoram to the filling and mix lightly together. Top the rolled dough with the filling, leaving a 2.5cm border of crust exposed around the edge. Roll out the second half of the dough, trim to a 30cm circle and place on top of the filling. Wet the edge of the bottom crust, then fold in over the top and crimp to seal. Use a fork to pierce several holes all over the torta to allow the steam to escape. Gently brush the torta all over with a little olive oil. Bake in the oven for about 30 minutes until crispy and golden, then remove and leave to cool slightly. Cut into wedges with a sharp knife and serve.

PG TIPS   You can make the tortas individually and vary the fillings – some of my favourites are mozzarella and artichoke or spinach and potato, but the variations are only limited by your imagination.

Mediterranean pisto pie
with tapenade and salmorejo sauce

A pisto is a typical Spanish-style ratatouille made with wonderfully colourful vegetables and bursting with flavour. Good on its own, I think when wrapped in flaky buttery pastry it is unbeatable. A classic salmorejo sauce completes this dish fit for any table. Tapenade is a spicy olive paste flavoured with capers and is available from supermarkets.

4 tablespoons olive oil

1 aubergine, cut into large dice

1 red onion, thinly sliced

4 garlic cloves, thinly sliced

2 courgettes, sliced

1 red pepper, deseeded and finely sliced

1 red chilli, deseeded and finely chopped

1 teaspoon picked fresh oregano

400g prepared puff pastry

3 tablespoons tapenade

little beaten egg

1 teaspoon sesame seeds

salt and freshly ground black pepper

for the salmorejo sauce

4 ripe tomatoes

1 onion, finely chopped

1 red chilli, deseeded and finely chopped

1 garlic clove, crushed

2 tablespoons olive oil

1 tablespoon white wine vinegar

1 tablespoon chopped fresh flat-leaf parsley

Heat the olive oil in a large frying pan and, when hot, add the aubergine and fry for 2–3 minutes. Add the remaining vegetables and fry over a moderate heat until all the vegetables are softened. Season to taste, add the oregano and mix well together. Leave to cool.

Preheat the oven to 200°C/400°F/gas mark 6. On a lightly floured surface, roll out half the pastry to a rectangle measuring about 25cm long and 20cm wide and transfer to a large baking sheet. Spread the tapenade over the pastry base, then spoon over the vegetables leaving a 2.5cm border around the edge. Roll out the remaining pastry to the same size and use to cover the first. Brush the edges with water or beaten egg, then press together to seal. Lightly mark squares on the pastry with the back of a knife, brush with beaten egg and sprinkle with sesame seeds. Place in the oven to bake for 30–35 minutes or until risen and golden brown.

Meanwhile, for the salmorejo sauce, cut the tomatoes in half and place them on a baking sheet. Bake for 15–20 minutes until charred on both sides (or place under a preheated hot grill), remove and leave to cool. When the tomatoes are cold, peel and deseed them and place in a small food processor with the remaining ingredients, except the parsley. Blend to a smooth sauce, season to taste, transfer to a bowl and add the parsley. Cut the pie into sections and serve with the salmorejo sauce.

PG TIPS   Some new potatoes and buttered fresh spinach with toasted pine nuts make a great accompaniment.

Potato and leek flamiche
with celeriac and carrot remoulade

Flamiche can be either a sweet or savoury tart from northern France. The best known variety is made with leeks, sometimes with the addition of a local strong cheese called maroilles (a particular favourite of mine). Flamiche is the Flemish word for cake.

300g prepared puff pastry

25g unsalted butter

200g new potatoes, peeled and thinly sliced to 1cm thick

400g small leeks, sliced

100ml crème fraîche (or double cream)

2 teaspoons Dijon mustard

1 tablespoon chopped fresh tarragon

1 free-range egg yolk mixed with 1 tablespoon water

salt, freshly ground black pepper and ground nutmeg

for the remoulade

1/2 small celeriac, peeled

1 Granny Smith apple, cored and peeled

1 carrot, peeled

100ml good-quality mayonnaise

1 teaspoon Dijon mustard

1 teaspoon lemon juice

10g small fresh tarragon leaves

salt and freshly ground black pepper

serves 6

Preheat the oven to 220ºC/425ºF/gas mark 7. Divide the pastry into two then roll it out about 5mm thick and cut out 2 x 25cm circles (using a 25cm plate as a guide). Prick both circles with a fork and chill in the fridge while you make the filling.

Melt the butter in a large saucepan, add the potato slices, leeks and 2 tablespoons of water, cover, and boil rapidly for 1 minute. Remove the lid, add the crème fraîche and mustard and cook for a further 5–6 minutes until the vegetables are tender and the cream all but gone. Remove from the heat and leave to cool. Add the tarragon and season well with salt, freshly ground pepper and ground nutmeg.

When cold, place the vegetable mixture in a dome shape on one of the pastry circles, leaving a 3cm border around the edge. Brush the edges with water. Top with the other pastry circle, lightly press together and, with a sharp small knife, make vertical cuts along the pastry edges. Transfer to a greased baking sheet. With a small sharp knife, score the top of the pie from the centre outwards, to create a spoke effect. Brush all over with the beaten egg and cook in the oven for 25–30 minutes until golden and flaky.

Meanwhile, for the remoulade, cut the celeriac, apple and carrot into fine strips or julienne on a kitchen mandolin. Place in a bowl, add the mayonnaise, salt, pepper and mustard and cream together gently – the vegetables and apple should bound in the mayonnaise. Finally add the lemon juice and mix again.

Cut the flamiche into wedges, garnish with the remoulade alongside and scatter the tarragon leaves over the top. Serve immediately.

PG TIPS   When using herbs in salads I rarely chop them, preferring to use small ones, leaving them whole to get the fullest of flavour from them.

Parsnip tatin
with pickled beetroots and onion confit

Delicious little individual savoury tatins of parsnip caramelised in a sweet and sour spice caramel, topped with pickled beetroot. Good parsnips are available all year round now, but I still find the best follow a winter cold snap to bring out their best flavour.

4 medium-sized parsnips, halved lengthways with
*   centre cores removed*
2 tablespoons olive oil
45g soft brown sugar
4 tablespoons white wine vinegar
juice of 1 lemon
1 teaspoon ground cumin
1 teaspoon preserved stem ginger, finely chopped
400g prepared puff pastry
2 pickled beetroots, drained and finely shredded
few mixed salad leaves
salt and freshly ground black pepper

for the onion confit
4 tablespoons olive oil
200g red onions, halved and sliced
1 teaspoon soft brown sugar
2 garlic cloves, crushed
pinch of red chilli flakes
1 teaspoon lemon thyme leaves (optional)

4 x 10cm square tins

Preheat the oven to 200°C/400°F/gas mark 6. Toss the parsnips with the olive oil in a roasting tin, season lightly and place in the oven to cook for 30 minutes, turning them occasionally.

For the onion confit, heat the oil in a frying pan, add the onions and cook over a moderate heat for 5–6 minutes or until starting to soften. Add the sugar, garlic and chilli flakes, lower the heat and add 4 tablespoons of water. Cook for 15 minutes until they become lightly caramelised and tender. Add the lemon thyme if desired. Remove the onions with a slotted spoon and leave to cool.

Heat the pan again over a high heat, add the sugar, vinegar, lemon juice, cumin and ginger and simmer for 6–8 minutes until caramelised. Add the roasted parsnip and roll in the glaze syrup for 1 minute. Remove and set aside.

Roll out the pastry to about 5mm thick, then using a 13cm cutter, cut out four rounds. Arrange the caramelised parsnips (cut-side up) in the bottom of the tins and spoon over any juices from the pan. Top with the onion confit, pressing down lightly, then lay the cut pastry rounds on top, press down and bake for 20 minutes or until golden and puffed. When cooked, leave to cool slightly before inverting them on to four serving plates. Drizzle over any remaining cooking juices and top with the pickled beetroot and salad leaves. Serve immediately.

Cauliflower singaras
with subj chaat and coriander chutney

Singaras, like their cousins samosas, are an everyday snack sold by street vendors in India. Enjoy them here with delicious accompaniments.

for the singaras

1 cauliflower, cut into florets

25g ghee or sunflower oil

1 small onion, finely chopped

1 garlic clove, crushed

1cm piece of root ginger, peeled and finely grated

1 small hot green chilli, finely chopped

1/2 teaspoon ground cumin

1/2 teaspoon ground coriander

1/2 teaspoon garam masala

3 tablespoons chopped fresh coriander

2 tablespoons chopped fresh mint

lemon juice

1 packet of samosa pastry

vegetable oil for deep-frying

salt and freshly ground black pepper

for the subj chaat

75g tamarind pulp

40g brown sugar, or to taste

2 red peppers, roasted, deseeded and cut into 1cm dice

1 yellow pepper, roasted, deseeded and cut into 1cm dice

100g pineapple, cut into 1cm dice

1 red onion, sliced

pinch of ground cumin

pinch of chaat masala

salt

for the coriander chutney

50g coriander, chopped

2 small green chillies, deseeded and chopped

3 tablespoons lemon juice

1/2 onion, chopped

2 tablespoons peanuts

Cook the cauliflower in boiling water for 6–8 minutes and remove with a slotted spoon into cold water. Drain and dry.

Heat the oil in a large frying pan, add the onion and garlic and fry over a moderate heat until lightly golden. Add the ginger and chilli and cook for 2–3 minutes. Add the cauliflower, cumin, coriander, garam masala and 100ml water and cook over a high heat until all the liquid has gone and the cauliflower is slightly mushy. Finally add the herbs, lemon juice and season to taste. Transfer to a bowl and leave to cool.

Using one strip of the pastry at a time, place 1 tablespoon of the filling mixture at one end. Diagonally fold up the pastry to form an enclosed triangle. Moisten the end of the strip with water and press lightly to secure. Prepare all the singaras in the same manner.

For the subj chaat, place the tamarind and 350ml water in a pan, bring to the boil and simmer for 10–12 minutes until the tamarind coats the base of a spoon. Add the sugar, or more to taste, and a little salt and leave to cool. Place the peppers, pineapple and onion in a bowl and add enough of the tamarind sauce to coat the mixture. Season with a little cumin and chaat masala.

Heat the oil in a small fryer or large pan to 170ºC/325ºF and fry the singaras in small batches until golden and crispy. Remove with a slotted spoon and drain on kitchen paper.

For the chutney, place all the ingredients together in a blender and blitz to a chunky consistency. The chutney will keep well in a storage jar in the fridge for 4–5 days.

Place a pile of the subj chaat on a plate, place the singaras on top and drizzle over a little of the chutney. Alternatively, serve separately.

Potato pizza bianco
with mozzarella, beetroot and rosemary

A tasty pizza-style flatbread made of mashed potato, topped with sweet beetroot and mozzarella cheese. It makes a great light lunch option or unusual vegetarian starter. Always use the best quality buffalo mozzarella you can find as there are many cheap inferior makes on the market – it will make such a difference.

for the flatbread

50g unsalted butter

125g self-raising flour

pinch of salt

225g hot, freshly cooked mashed potato

1 free-range egg, beaten

for the topping

2 buffalo mozzarella, thinly sliced

2 medium-sized beetroots, roasted (see page 77)
  and peeled

2 tablespoons olive oil

1 teaspoon fresh rosemary, roughly chopped

100ml crème fraîche

Preheat the oven to 220°C/425°F/gas mark 7. In a bowl, rub the butter with the flour, add a pinch of salt and the hot mashed potato and lightly bind together. Turn the mixture out onto a lightly floured surface and knead it lightly. Using a floured rolling pin, roll out the dough into a large circle approximately 1cm thick. Using a floured cookie cutter, cut out 4 x 12.5cm circles, then brush them liberally all over with beaten egg.

Place the potato flatbreads on a large well greased baking tray and lay the mozzarella slices evenly over each flatbread. Slice the beetroots thinly and place on top. Sprinkle over the olive oil and rosemary and place in the oven to bake for 15–18 minutes or until the potato bases are golden and crispy. To serve, top with a good dollop of crème fraîche.

Quail's eggs béarnaise tartlets
with mushroom and olive duxelles and asparagus au beurre

A delicious rich, buttery herb sauce coating soft-boiled quail's eggs in a crisp pastry tart shell. An impressive starter for a special occasion dinner party.

300g prepared shortcrust pastry

12 quail's eggs

12 cooked asparagus tips, halved lengthways

15g unsalted butter

salt and freshly ground black pepper

for the mushroom and olive duxelles

15g unsalted butter

1 shallot, finely chopped

1 teaspoon fresh thyme leaves

175g flat mushrooms, finely chopped

25g stoned black olives, finely chopped

1 teaspoon honey

100ml dry white wine

30g fresh white breadcrumbs

salt and freshly ground black pepper

for the béarnaise sauce

2 tablespoons white wine vinegar

2 tablespoons water

1/2 teaspoon crushed white peppercorns

3 free-range egg yolks

175g unsalted butter, clarified (see PG TIPS)

2 tablespoons chopped fresh tarragon

1 tablespoon chopped fresh flat-leaf parsley

salt and freshly ground black pepper

4 x 9.5cm tartlet tins

Preheat the oven to 190°C/375°F/gas mark 5. Roll out the pastry to line the tartlet tins. Fill with baking paper and baking beans and bake blind for 10 minutes. Remove the beans and paper and return to the oven for a further 5 minutes. Leave to cool.

For the mushroom and olive duxelles, heat the butter in a frying pan, add the shallots and thyme and cook for 1 minute. Add the mushrooms, olives and honey and cook for 4–5 minutes until golden brown. Add the wine and cook for a further 1 minute. Finally add the breadcrumbs, mix well, season to taste and keep warm.

For the béarnaise sauce, place the vinegar, water and peppercorns in a small pan and boil vigorously until it has reduced to 1 tablespoon. Remove from the heat and leave to cool, then strain into a heatproof bowl. Add the egg yolks to the liquid and whisk together. Set the bowl over a pan of simmering water, with the base just above the water. Whisk the egg mixture for 5–6 minutes or until it becomes thick and ribbon-like, creamy and smooth in texture. Remove from the heat and slowly add the butter in a thin stream, whisking until the sauce is thick and glossy. Add the herbs and season to taste. Keep warm over a bain marie.

Boil the quail's eggs for 2 minutes in boiling water, then immediately remove them with a slotted spoon and plunge in cold water to refresh them. While they are still warm, carefully peel them.

To finish the dish, fill each tartlet shell with some olive and mushroom duxelles and top each with three quail's eggs. Coat the eggs completely with béarnaise sauce, then place under a hot grill to glaze for about 30 seconds until beautifully golden. Heat the asparagus tips in hot butter and season to taste. Place a line of asparagus tips on each plate, top with an egg-filled tartlet and serve. Delicious!

PG TIPS   If you want to prepare your quail's eggs in advance, a little tip is to cook them as usual, then immerse them directly into a mixture of cold water and some distilled vinegar and leave for 10 minutes before peeling. To serve, simply reheat for 15 seconds in boiling water.

To clarify butter, heat the butter in a pan until bubbling and skim off any impurities that rise to the surface with a ladle or large spoon. Slowly pour off the liquid butter, leaving the milky white sediment in the pan. It is now ready for use.

Kadaifi apple fritters
with pickled blue cheese salad

Kadaifi (or kataifi) is a type of filo pastry that is finely shredded and makes an interesting wrapping for many dishes. It is available from Middle Eastern or Greek stores. Yorkshire Blue is a creamy blue cheese available in supermarkets.

for the kadaifi fritters

1 Granny Smith apple, cored and finely diced

juice of 1/2 lemon

125g Yorkshire blue cheese (or other creamy blue cheese), crumbled

1/2 teaspoon Dijon mustard

pinch of paprika

175g fresh white breadcrumbs

1 free-range egg yolk

little flour

100g kadaifi pastry

40g unsalted butter, melted

vegetable oil for deep-frying

salt, freshly ground black pepper and ground nutmeg

for the pickled blue cheese salad

2 tablespoons caster sugar

4 tablespoons red wine vinegar

1 carrot, peeled

75g celeriac, peeled

1 red onion, peeled and thinly sliced

75g baby spinach leaves

30g fresh flat-leaf parsley leaves

50g rocket leaves

75g Yorkshire blue cheese, frozen for 10 minutes and shaved

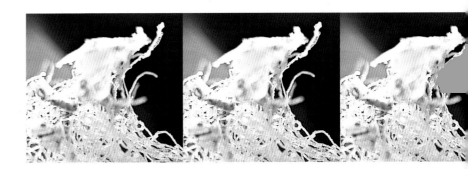

Coat the apple with the lemon juice and toss together for 1 minute.

For the kadaifi, place the crumbled cheese in a bowl and add the diced apple, the mustard, paprika and breadcrumbs and finally the egg yolk. Season and bring the mixture together to a thick paste that holds its shape. Refrigerate for 2 hours, then remove and shape into eight small patties. Dust with a little flour.

Carefully unwrap the pastry and spread it out onto a work surface. Liberally brush the pastry strands with melted butter, then wrap the patties in it ensuring the pastry completely covers them. Set aside.

For the salad, heat the sugar and vinegar in a pan and boil for 1 minute. Using a kitchen mandolin or sharp knife, shred the carrot and celeriac in a bowl and add the thinly sliced onion. Pour over the hot vinegar and leave to cool. When cold, add the spinach, parsley and rocket and toss well together. Finally add half the cheese.

To serve, deep- or shallow-fry the kadaifi fritters for about 3–4 minutes until golden and crispy, remove and drain on kitchen paper. Divide the salad and pile high on four plates, place two fritters per person on top of each salad and sprinkle over the remaining shaved cheese. Alternatively serve the salad separately.

Open-faced spinach and feta sambusak
with preserved lemon salsa

Preserving lemons in salt is commonplace in Middle Eastern countries and it adds spicy overtones to the lemon's sourness. They are easy to prepare at home but take a while to mature (up to three months). However, there are some good-quality ones on the market.

for the sambusak

2 tablespoons olive oil

50g pine nuts

1 large onion, thinly sliced

1 teaspoon allspice

1/2 teaspoon cumin seeds

200g spinach, washed

120g sunblush tomatoes, chopped

1/2 teaspoon lemon zest

300g prepared puff pastry

175g Greek feta cheese, crumbled

little beaten egg

salt and freshly ground black pepper

for the preserved lemon salsa

3 tablespoons extra-virgin olive oil

juice of 2 lemons

1 garlic clove, crushed

1 small red pepper, halved, deseeded and
    cut into 1cm dice

1 red onion, finely chopped

1/2 cucumber, deseeded and cut into 1cm dice

1 teaspoon preserved lemon, cut into 3mm dice

3 tablespoons chopped fresh coriander

2 plum tomatoes, cut into 1cm dice

pinch of sugar

salt and freshly ground black pepper

Preheat the oven to 190°C/375°F/gas mark 5. Heat the olive oil in a frying pan and, when hot, add the pine nuts and cook until golden all over. Remove and drain, reserving the oil. Return the oil to the pan on the heat, add the onion and cook over a moderate heat for about 8–10 minutes until golden all over. Add the allspice and cumin seeds, cook for a further 1 minute, remove with a slotted spoon and set aside.

Once again return the pan to the heat, add the spinach and cook for 3–4 minutes until wilted and all the excess moisture absorbed. Return the onions and nuts to the pan and add the sunblush tomatoes. Cook together for a further 2 minutes. Add the lemon zest, season to taste and set aside to cool.

Roll out the pastry 5mm thick, then cut out 4 x 9cm circles. Lay out the circles on a flat surface, then divide the spinach mixture equally between them. Divide the feta into four equal amounts and place on top of the spinach. Brush the edges of the pastry with the beaten egg and bring them up to the centre, pressing them lightly, leaving the centre of the pastry open. Place the sambusaks on a non-stick baking sheet and place in the oven for 15–20 minutes until golden and flaky.

Meanwhile, for the salsa, mix the olive oil, lemon juice and garlic in a bowl. Add the remaining ingredients, toss well together and season to taste. To serve, place the sambusaks on to four serving plates and dress with the salsa dressing. It is important to eat the sambusaks warm while the cheese remains soft and creamy.

Portobello tart gratin
in hazelnut pastry with parsley and garlic sauce

Any combination of mushroom, garlic and parsley is always a winner. If
fontina cheese is unavailable, use an alternative easy melting cheese such
as emmental or gruyère.

for the portobello tart

150g plain flour

100g ground hazelnuts

175g unsalted butter, chilled and cut into small dice

1 small free-range egg, lightly beaten

1 garlic clove

2 tablespoons olive oil

8 medium-sized portobello mushrooms, with stems

1 shallot, finely chopped

1 teaspoon fresh thyme leaves

50g fontina cheese, thinly sliced

20g fresh flat-leaf parsley leaves, chopped

salt and freshly ground black pepper

for the parsley and garlic sauce

25g fresh flat-leaf parsley leaves

1 garlic clove, crushed

100ml single cream

100ml vegetable stock

25g unsalted butter, chilled and cut into small pieces

salt and freshly ground black pepper

For the pastry, place the flour, salt and hazelnuts in a bowl, add the chilled diced butter and work with your fingertips until it resembles breadcrumbs. Add the egg and work it into a dough, kneading gently. Refrigerate for 30 minutes.

Preheat the oven to 200°C/400°F/gas mark 6. Clean the mushrooms with a wet cloth and cut in half vertically through the stems to yield sixteen halves. Crush the garlic clove with the blade of a knife. Rub the inside of a large non-stick pan all over with the garlic clove, then discard it. Heat the oil in the pan and, when hot, add the mushrooms, shallot and thyme and fry over a high heat until golden all over. Season to taste and keep warm.

Roll out the pastry 5mm thick, then cut into 4 x 10cm long x 5cm wide strips. Place on a baking sheet and bake in the oven for 10–12 minutes. Remove and top each cooked strip with some fontina cheese slices, then top each with the mushrooms. Return to the oven for 2 minutes.

For the sauce, place the parsley and garlic in a small food processor and blend to a purée. Add the cream and stock, then blend again until very smooth. Heat in a pan with the butter until boiling and season to taste. Place the tarts on to four serving plates and spoon around the parsley and garlic sauce. Sprinkle the chopped parsley over the mushrooms and serve immediately.

Desserts

There is nothing more pleasing, I am told by enthusiastic home cooks, than creating 5-star desserts in the home. Desserts may be the parting memory of any great dinner party, but from my experience, they are the most desired and anticipated offering of all the courses.

I have given you some unusual, yet accessible, dishes here to give that wow factor to the end of a meal.

Lavender yogurt cheesecake
with kaffir lime-flavoured strawberries

A simple and delightful summer dessert. Everyone loves cheesecake in one form or another – here lavender adds a touch of summer elegance.

for the kaffir lime-flavoured strawberries

125g caster sugar

zest and juice of 2 limes

6 kaffir lime leaves, torn

225g fresh strawberries, hulled

50g unsalted butter

1/2 teaspoon dried lavender flowers, finely crushed (plus some lavender sprigs for decorating)

120g sweet digestive biscuits, finely crushed

80g caster sugar

250g good-quality cream cheese

250ml thick set natural yogurt

175ml double cream

20cm flan ring

For the strawberries, bring the sugar and 225ml water to the boil, ensuring the sugar has completely melted and formed a light syrup. Add the lime zest and juice and kaffir lime leaves and leave to cool. Halve the strawberries, place in a bowl and pour over the lime syrup. Refrigerate overnight.

For the cheesecake, melt the butter in a pan, add the lavender flowers and remove from the heat. Stir in the crushed biscuits and 30g sugar and mix well together. While still warm, press the biscuits into the base of a flan ring. Refrigerate for 2 hours to set.

In a bowl, beat the cream cheese, the remaining sugar and yogurt until smooth.

In another bowl, whip the double cream until half whipped and just holding its shape, then gently fold into the yogurt mixture until amalgamated. Spread the mixture over the lavender biscuit base and smooth over the surface with a palette knife. Return to the fridge for 1 hour or until easy to serve. Decorate the cheesecake with marinated strawberries and fresh lavender.

Soft cheese panna cotta
with pineapple and raspberries

Brillat-Savarin is a soft French triple-cream cheese and very moreish. It is creamy in texture, which makes it ideal for panna cotta. For me, Del Monte pineapples are the juiciest and sweetest, but they are expensive.

300ml double cream

1 vanilla pod, split with seeds removed and reserved

1 piece of lemon peel

125g caster sugar

6g vege-gel

300g soft Brillat-Savarin cheese

1/2 fresh pineapple, skin removed

150g sugar

3 tablespoons Malibu liqueur

175g fresh raspberries

1 teaspoon chopped pistachios (optional)

6 x 100g moulds or cups

serves 6

Place the cream in a pan with the vanilla pod, seeds, lemon peel and sugar. Heat until boiling, then remove and leave to infuse for 20 minutes. Remove the vanilla pod and lemon peel from the cream and sprinkle over the vege-gel. Slowly reheat the cream, whisking well and constantly until the mixture thickens. Remove from the heat, whisk in the cheese, then quickly pour into six oiled moulds or cups. Leave to cool, then refrigerate overnight to set.

For the fruits, cut the pineapple into small pieces. Bring 150ml water and the sugar to the boil, remove from the heat and leave to go cold. Add the Malibu liqueur, pineapple and raspberries and chill for 1 hour.

To serve, loosen the panna cotta from the moulds and place on individual serving plates. Decorate with the fruit and pistachios.

Banana tofu fool
with green tea sorbet and chocolate sauce

An interesting dessert for tofu lovers. Green tea is served in Japanese homes as a sign of welcome and is becoming increasingly popular in Britain. It is wonderful when infused into a sorbet, as used in this dessert.

for the green tea sorbet

50g caster sugar

30g glucose

10g green tea leaves (or powder)

for the banana tofu fool

125g silken tofu

100ml soy milk

1/2 teaspoon vanilla extract

200g Greek natural yogurt

2 bananas, peeled and chopped

zest and juice of 1 lemon

fresh mint leaves

for the chocolate sauce

50g good-quality bitter chocolate (70% cocoa solids)

125ml double cream

1/2 teaspoon vanilla extract

4 martini glasses or serving dishes

For the green tea sorbet, place 450ml water, the sugar and glucose in a pan and bring slowly to the boil. Remove from the heat, stir in the tea powder and stir until dissolved (or if using leaves just stir), remove from the heat and leave to infuse until cold, then strain. Transfer to an ice-cream maker and freeze according to the manufacturer's instructions. Place in a container and freeze until required.

For the banana tofu fool, place the tofu in a food processor and blend until smooth, then add the soy milk and vanilla extract and transfer to a bowl. Place the yogurt, chopped banana, lemon zest and juice in the food processor and blend until smooth. Fold the banana mixture into the tofu mixture and then spoon it into the serving dishes. Refrigerate to set for up to 4 hours.

For the chocolate sauce, break up the chocolate and place in a small pan with the cream and vanilla extract. Warm it gently, stirring lightly until smooth and creamy, then remove and leave to cool.

To serve, place a ball of green tea sorbet on the top of the fool, spoon over the chocolate sauce and decorate with mint.

Iced ricotta parfait
with caramelised peppers

I first saw sweet peppers being used in a dessert in New York some years ago. Chef David Burke of the Avenue Park Café in the Big Apple prepared an orange and strawberry tart with caramelised peppers for us – it was wonderful and a novel way of using peppers in a dessert preparation.

for the iced ricotta parfait

50g caster sugar

2 free-range eggs, separated

1 vanilla pod, split lengthways, seeds removed and reserved

250ml double cream

100g ricotta cheese

75ml Frangelico liqueur

zest of 1 lemon

hazelnut brittle (see PG TIPS) – optional

for the caramelised peppers

1 small red pepper, deseeded and cut into 1cm dice

1 yellow pepper, deseeded and cut into 1cm dice

4 tablespoons honey

1 teaspoon balsamic vinegar

juice of 1/2 lemon

50g soaked raisins, drained and dried

3 fresh tarragon leaves, chopped

6–8 small ramekins, soufflé dishes or 8 metal kitchen rings

serves 6–8

For the parfait (best made a day in advance), whisk together the sugar, egg yolks and vanilla seeds in a bowl until pale and almost doubled in volume. Half whip the cream until soft peaks begin to form (do not over-whisk). In another bowl, whisk the egg whites until very stiff peaks form. Add the cheese, liqueur and lemon zest to the egg yolks and blend together. Gently fold in the whipped cream, then fold in the egg whites. Spoon the mixture into 6–8 chosen dishes. Cover with clingfilm and freeze until required – at least 3 hours.

For the peppers, place them in a small pan with the honey and lightly caramelise them for 3–4 minutes until soft and tender. Add the vinegar, lemon juice, raisins and tarragon and cook together for 5 minutes to form a light syrup. Remove from the heat and leave to cool. To serve, remove the parfaits from their moulds by quickly immersing them half way up in hot water, then turn them out on to individual serving plate. Leave to soften for 5 minutes. Pour the pepper syrup over the parfaits and serve immediately. Decorate with the nut brittle, if desired.

PG TIPS   A simply prepared nut brittle makes a nice contrast to the parfait. Simply spread 50g peeled and chopped hazelnuts out on a lightly oiled oven tray. Combine 100g caster sugar with 2 tablespoons of water in a pan and stir over a moderate heat until the sugar is dissolved. Bring to the boil and cook without stirring, until caramelised and golden. Remove from the heat, allow the bubbles to subside and pour over the hazelnuts. Set aside to harden and go cold. When hard, roughly crush the pieces. This brittle can be made and stored successfully in an airtight container for 1 week.

Gooseberry clafoutis

with black olive ice cream

Ever since I first experienced sweet syrupy cooked olives in the south of France some years ago, there has been no stopping my imagination running riot. Here the candied olives are made into an unusual ice cream, which contrasts beautifully with the warm clafoutis.

for the black olive ice cream

100g black olives, stoned

100g sugar

250ml full-fat milk

350ml whipping cream

6 free-range egg yolks

for the gooseberry clafoutis

2 free-range eggs

2 free-range egg yolks

80g caster sugar

30g cornflour

100ml full-fat milk

200ml whipping cream

1/2 vanilla pod, seeds removed and reserved

50g unsalted butter, melted

zest of 1/2 lemon

475g slightly under-ripe gooseberries

little icing sugar to dust

Prepare the olive ice cream a day in advance. Cook the olives for 5 minutes in boiling water and then drain. Repeat this process three times to remove any bitterness from the olives and then chop finely. Place 50g of the sugar along with 150ml water in a pan and slowly bring to the boil, raise the heat, add the chopped olives and cook for about 10 minutes until jam-like in consistency. Remove and set aside.

Preheat the oven to 180°C/350°F/gas mark 4. Heat the milk and cream in a pan along with the candied olives until almost boiling point, leave to infuse over a low heat without boiling for 10 minutes. Beat the egg yolks and remaining sugar in a bowl until light and fluffy, then gradually whisk the olive cream into the egg mixture. Return to the pan, stirring constantly over a low heat until the mixture thickens sufficiently to coat the back of a spoon. Do not let it boil or it will curdle. Remove from the heat and, when cool, refrigerate, then freeze in an ice-cream machine according to the manufacturer's instructions.

For the gooseberry clafoutis, place the eggs, egg yolks and 30g sugar in a bowl and beat until light. Gradually add the cornflour and beat to a smooth batter. Add the milk, cream, vanilla seeds and 25g melted butter. Beat again until smooth. Put the remaining melted butter and sugar in a pan, add the gooseberries, lemon zest and 100ml water and cook for 8–10 minutes or until the gooseberries are just soft. Divide the gooseberries between four gratin-style dishes and then pour over an equal amount of the batter into each dish. Place in the oven to cook for 20–25 minutes until golden but still light and soft inside. Dust with icing sugar and serve with the black olive ice cream.

Honey-roasted fruits

with rosemary and pear rosti

This is an ideal fruit dessert for the colder months. The fruits absorb the flavours of honey and rosemary as they cook, giving off a wonderful aroma which pervades the room. Serve with some crème fraîche mixed with some fresh vanilla seeds or extract.

for the pear rosti

2 pears

50ml maple syrup

2 egg yolks

20g ground semolina

15g unsalted butter

3 tablespoons caster sugar

40g unsalted butter

3 tablespoons whole blanched almonds

75ml clear honey

150g seedless white grapes (preferably Muscat)

*150g dried apricots, soaked in water for 1 hour
    and drained*

*100g dried prunes, soaked in water for 1 hour
    and drained*

45ml cognac

juice of $^1/2$ lemon

*1 teaspoon chopped fresh rosemary (plus a little more
    to decorate)*

vanilla crème fraîche (optional)

For the pear rosti, peel the pears, remove the cores and grate them coarsely. Dry in a cloth to squeeze out all the juice. Place in a bowl and add the syrup, egg yolks and ground semolina to the pear. Mix well together and shape into four flat cakes. Melt the butter and fry the rosti until golden on both sides. Keep warm.

In a small frying pan, heat the sugar with 1 teaspoon of water for about 5 minutes, until melted and golden. Whisk in half of the butter, add the almonds and cook until caramelised in the sugar. Remove the almonds and set aside.

Melt the remaining butter in another larger frying pan, add the honey and bring to the boil. Add the grapes, apricots and prunes and coat them evenly. Add the cognac and carefully ignite. Once the flames die out, add the lemon juice and rosemary and simmer gently until the sauce thickens.

Place one pear rosti in each dessert bowl, pour around the fruits and sprinkle over the caramelised almonds. Garnish each with some rosemary and a good dollop of vanilla crème fraîche, if desired. Serve immediately.

Spice-roasted nectarines
with pistachio milk sauce

A refreshing dessert packed with flavour, ideal for the hot summer
months when nectarines are ripe, juicy and plentiful.

4 large firm but ripe nectarines

40g unsalted butter

10 black peppercorns, cracked

1/2 teaspoon Szechuan peppercorns

1/2 teaspoon dried pink peppercorns

1/2 teaspoon ground star anise

30g caster sugar

2 tablespoons kirsch

for the pistachio milk sauce

1 small tin condensed milk

30g peeled pistachios

1 tablespoon kirsch

4 scoops of good-quality vanilla ice cream

Preheat the oven to 230°C/450°F/gas mark 8. Cut the nectarines in half, twist and separate and remove the centre stones. To remove the skins, place in a pan of boiling water for about 4 minutes – the skins will start to wrinkle and fall off. Remove the skins and place the nectarine halves in an ovenproof baking dish.

Melt the butter in a non-stick frying pan, add the spices and cook for 1 minute. Add the sugar and 100ml water and lightly caramelise together; add the kirsch. Pour the syrup over the nectarines and place in the oven to roast for 5–6 minutes.

Meanwhile for the sauce, place the condensed milk, pistachios and kirsch in a food processor and blend until smooth.

To serve, pour a little pool of pistachio sauce in the centre of each serving plate or shallow bowl, add two nectarine halves, top with 1 scoop of ice cream and pour over the pan syrup.

Sauces and stocks

As with all good cooking, perfection lies in getting the basic techniques right, none more so than when using a vegetable stock in a recipe. Poorly made vegetable stock can taste like dishwater and lack body and depth of flavour. Here are the stock and sauce bases used for this book that will help you ensure success every time. For those people who find stockmaking a tedious job, using a vegetable stock cube is fine, but some can be a little salty in flavour – take time to taste them made-up before use.

Light vegetable stock for soups and sauces

little olive oil

6 large carrots, peeled and sliced

4 sticks of celery, chopped

2 leeks, chopped

3 large onions, chopped

2 heads of garlic, halved horizontally

1 large turnip, chopped

small bunch of fresh flat-leaf parsley

small bunch of fresh thyme

small bunch of fresh coriander

2 bay leaves

8 black peppercorns

4 litres water

makes 2 litres

Heat a very large heavy-based pan with a little olive oil, add the vegetables, cover with a lid and sweat for 5 minutes. Add the herbs and spices, cover with water and simmer gently for 40–45 minutes or until the vegetables are soft. Strain carefully through a fine strainer, leave to cool and store until needed.

Roasted vegetable stock for sauce bases

50g dried wild mushrooms (or fresh mushrooms)

4 large shallots, chopped

2 red peppers, deseeded and chopped

6 large carrots, peeled and chopped

2 leeks, chopped

2 garlic cloves, halved horizontally

little olive oil

2 tablespoons tomato purée

small bunch of fresh thyme

400g tinned tomatoes, chopped

4 litres water

makes 2 litres

Preheat the oven to 220°C/425°F/gas mark 7. Divide the mushrooms, shallots, peppers, carrots, leeks and garlic between two large baking tins. Drizzle a little olive oil over the vegetables and toss them well to ensure an even coating. Place in the oven to roast and lightly caramelise for about 30 minutes, turning them regularly as they roast. Remove, stir in a little tomato purée into each tin of vegetables, mix well and return to the oven for a further 10 minutes. Remove and transfer to a large pan, add the thyme, chopped tomatoes and cover with water. Simmer for 40 minutes. Strain carefully through a fine strainer, leave to cool and store until needed.

Roasted vegetable reduction (vegetarian jus or vegetarian wine sauce)

4 tablespoons olive oil

50g unsalted butter

4 shallots, chopped

2 carrots, peeled and chopped

4 sticks of celery, chopped

6 garlic cloves, halved horizontally

500g button mushrooms, chopped

sprig of fresh thyme

1 tablespoon tomato purée

2 tablespoons plain flour

100ml red wine

4 litres roasted vegetable stock (see above)

1 tablespoon vegetarian Worcestershire sauce

300ml Madeira or sherry

makes 2 litres

Heat the olive oil and butter in a large heavy-based pan, add the shallots, carrots, celery and garlic and cook over a low heat for about 10–15 minutes until golden and lightly caramelised. Add the mushrooms and thyme and cook for a further 2–3 minutes. Stir in the tomato purée, cook for 1 minute, then mix in the flour and cook over a low heat for 2 minutes. Pour over the red wine, roasted vegetable stock and Worcestershire sauce, stir and bring to the boil. Add the Madeira, simmer for 20 minutes and then strain into a clean bowl, discarding the vegetables. Leave to cool and store until needed.

This sauce may be varied by changing the wine used, such as marsala or white wine. This sauce should be finished with a knob of butter before serving, which not only adds richness but also a wonderful shiny gloss to the sauce.

Index

Conversion tables

Volume

5ml	1 teaspoon
10ml	1 dessert spoon
15ml	1 tablespoon
30ml	1fl oz
50ml	2fl oz
75ml	3fl oz
100ml	3½fl oz
125ml	4fl oz
150ml	5fl oz (¼ pint)
200ml	7fl oz (⅓ pint)
250ml (0.25 litre)	9fl oz
300ml	10fl oz (½ pint)
350ml	12fl oz
400ml	14fl oz
425ml	15fl oz (¾ pint)
450ml	16fl oz
500ml (0.5 litre)	18fl oz
600ml	1 pint (20fl oz)
700ml	1¼ pints
850ml	1½ pints
1 litre	1¾ pints
1.2 litres	2 pints
1.5 litres	2½ pints
1.8 litres	3 pints
2 litres	3½ pints

Weight

10g	½oz
20g	¾oz
25g	1oz
50g	2oz
60g	2½oz
75g	3oz
100g	3½oz
110g	4oz (¼lb)
150g	5oz
175g	6oz
200g	7oz
225g	8oz (½lb)
250g (¼kg)	9oz
275g	10oz
350g	12oz (¾lb)
400g	14oz
450g	1lb
500g (½kg)	18oz
600g	1¼lb
700g	1½lb
900g	2lb
1kg	2¼lb
1.1kg	2½lb
1.3kg	3lb
1.5kg	3lb 5oz

Measurements

3mm	⅛in
5mm	¼in
1cm	½in
2cm	¾in
2.5cm	1in
3cm	1¼in
4cm	1½in
5cm	2in
6cm	2½in
7.5cm	2¾in
9cm	3½in
10cm	4in
11.5cm	4½in
12.5cm	5in
15cm	6in
17cm	6½in
18cm	7in
20.5cm	8in
23cm	9in
24cm	9½in
25.5cm	10in
30.5cm	11in

Acknowledgements
This book could not have happened without the collaboration of three very dear friends: To Kyle Cathie for giving me yet another opportunity to express my food in print. I thank you and your wonderful team for your support and encouragement. To Linda Tubby, home economist, and Gus Filgate, photographer, for yet another ultimate display of professionalism. Thank you so much as a team you are unbeatable.

And also: To Vanessa Courtier, for her excellent design which perfectly expresses the spirit of this book. To Penny Markham, for sourcing some wonderful props for photography. To Jane Middleton, for checking text, typography and style. To Lara King and her trusty PC, great job as usual, thank you! To my agents, Limelight Management, for their tireless support and friendship. Last but most importantly, project editor Sophie Allen at Kyle Cathie for her calm, methodical approach at all times, but more importantly, her enthusiasm for the project since its initiation.